Even If

Trusting God When The Unthinkable Happens

Ronald L. Glenn

Sigfam Media Group
P.O. Box 27
Wilberforce, OH 45384
http://www.sigfam.com

Cover and graphic designs by Rev. Samuel A. Harris, Jr.

Acknowledgments

The author is especially grateful to Drs. Michelle Daniels and Janie S. Glenn for significant editorial assistance and to Rev. Samuel A. Harris, Jr. and Jason S. Glenn for their usual excellent work with graphics and document layout.

Dedication

This book is dedicated to the Rev. Dr. Faye Taylor, the Rev. Melonie A. Valentine, and the many other servants in ministry who pledged to be faithful to their vows even if...

Contents

Preface

I was asked by a friend to explain the symbolism on the cover of this book. He wondered in particular about the sword with the single drop of blood on its tip. I told him that I wanted to evoke the idea of pending danger that can only be stayed by the hand of God. The single drop of blood is a reminder that sometimes God allows the sword to find its target. God heals but many faithful servants of God have heard the dreaded diagnosis of cancer. God protects but automobiles crash anyway. God loves little children but sometimes our most precious ones are abused. The drop of blood also reminds us that even Jesus felt the sword as it drew blood. He prayed that he might not have to drink from the bitter cup of torture and death but his trust in God was so complete that he could declare, *not my will but yours.* (Luke 22:42).

What are we Christians to think when the unthinkable happens? The process involves two steps. First, we must develop the faith to believe that God is able. Second, we must put our complete trust in God. This helps us to reach Job's resolution of this tension— *though he slay me, yet will I trust him.* (Job 13:15). The three Hebrew slaves in Chapter 1 spoke the words that led to the title of this book, *My God is able but even if he does not...* Each succeeding chapter examines another exposure to the tension and uncertainty of the tenuous situations in life that force us to reach the place where we can declare for ourselves, *even if...*

Chapter 1

Even If

If we are thrown into the blazing furnace, the God we serve is able to save us from it, and he will rescue us from your hand, O king. But even if he does not, we want you to know, O king, that we will not serve your gods or worship the image of gold you have set up. (Daniel 3:17-18).

The scriptures about the three Hebrew boys in the fiery furnace and Daniel in the lion's den are two of the most well-known of the Hebrew Scriptures. However, a true appreciation of these scriptures requires that one must understand some basic facts about biblical history and theology. Some of these historical lessons are very discomforting and painful.

The kingdom had been divided into parts following the death of Solomon amidst squabbles among his sons and heirs. Jehoiakim, the king of the southern kingdom, Judah, was defeated by Nebuchadnezzar, king of Babylon. The Babylonians took some sacred items from the temple of God and placed them in their own pagan temple. They also took something else from the kingdom of Judah. *Then the king ordered Ashpenaz, chief of his court officials, to bring in some of the Israelites from the royal family and the nobility--young men without any physical defect, handsome, showing aptitude for every kind of learning, well informed, quick to understand, and qualified to serve in the king's palace. He was to teach them the language and literature of the Babylonians. The king assigned them a daily amount of food and wine from the king's table. They were to be trained for three years, and after that they were to enter the king's service.* (Daniel 1:3-5).

The Babylonians took the brightest, best looking and most intelligent young men from among the Hebrew people and prepared them for the king's service. The polite translation of the scriptures masks a grim and painful part of the preparation process. My sisters, if you are sitting next to a man who is very special to you, take his arm and pat his hand gently as you read the next section of this chapter. The young men without any physical defect were made defective in the most painful way through castration. Many scholars believe that Daniel and the other Hebrew boys were eunuchs.

These scriptures are hard to read as we reflect on their deeper meanings and apply them to our modern-day situations. Captive, enslaved and oppressed peoples have long bemoaned the loss of their young men. The Babylonians followed several key steps in the preparation process beyond the infamous neutering operation. First, he *was to teach them the language and literature of the Babylonians,* (Daniel 1:4). Second, they gave the boys a special diet which they refused to eat, preferring instead the healthy diet revealed to them by God. *The king assigned them a daily amount of food and wine from the king's table.* (Daniel 1:5). Then, they changed their names. *The chief official gave them new names: to Daniel, the name Belteshazzar; to Hananiah, Shadrach; to Mishael, Meshach; and to Azariah, Abednego,* (Daniel 1:7).

Learning the language and literature of the oppressor also means forgetting the native language and literature of the captive people. The change in diet seems harmless enough but was actually part of the process of separation from the former culture. Eating from the king's table was in principle designed to make the new slaves have a healthy appearance that looked like that of the captors. It also may have been part of their unspoken duty of testing the king's food to guard against assassins who chose poison as their weapon.

Then, to complete the transformation, they stripped them of their Hebrew names and gave them Babylonian names. *The chief official gave them new names: to Daniel, the name Belteshazzar; to Hananiah, Shadrach; to Mishael, Meshach; and to Azariah, Abednego,* (Daniel 1:7). I have met many international transplants to America who softly complain about the refusal of Americans to learn to pronounce their names and their insistence that they take on new American names or Americanized versions of their original names.

To these four young men God gave knowledge and understanding of all kinds of literature and learning. And Daniel could understand visions and dreams of all kinds. (Daniel 1:17). These God-given abilities provided the first opportunity for Daniel and his Hebrew companions to show the awesome power of God. *In the second year of his reign, Nebuchadnezzar had dreams; his mind was troubled and he could not sleep. The king asked Daniel (also called Belteshazzar), "Are you able to tell me what I saw in my dream and interpret it?" Daniel replied, "No wise man, enchanter, magician or diviner can explain to the king the mystery he has asked about, but there is a God in heaven who reveals mysteries",* (Daniel 2:1, 26-28).

Daniel did not forget his friends. He understood that they were all in this situation together. When he was elevated for interpreting the king's dreams, he spoke a word for his friends and they too enjoyed the benefits of the king's favor. *Then the king placed Daniel in a high position and lavished many gifts on him. He made him ruler over the entire province of Babylon and placed him in charge of all its wise men. Moreover, at Daniel's request the king appointed Shadrach, Meshach and Abednego administrators over the province of Babylon, while Daniel himself remained at the royal court,* (Daniel 2:48-49).

These young Hebrew men had reached the pinnacle of administration in the oppressive society that captured them. They never forgot that they enjoyed the favor of the king because they enjoyed the favor of God. They never denied their God. Daniel gave an important lesson to the Christians of today about how they can be faithful to God in the midst of an increasingly secular and anti-religious society. The king decided that everyone must bow down and worship the image of gold. Anyone who failed to worship the image would be thrown into the fiery furnace and killed. *Then the herald loudly proclaimed, "This is what you are commanded to do, O peoples, nations and men of every language: As soon as you hear the sound of the horn, flute, zither, lyre, harp, pipes and all kinds of music, you must fall down and worship the image of gold that King Nebuchadnezzar has set up. Whoever does not fall down and worship will immediately be thrown into a blazing furnace,"* (Daniel 3:4-6).

Of course, the Hebrews did not bow down. They took a stand for righteousness and faithfulness to their God. We are called to do no less today. When science says bow down before the altar of evolution, Christians must say "no" and stand for the Creator God who is in fact responsible for the universe. When abortion rights advocates demand that we bow before the altar of death for unborn infants, we must stand for the God-given obligation to sustain life for every child conceived. When power-mad despots demand that we bow before them and their malevolent rule, we must remind them that God is still on the throne and is the only one that we serve.

Be warned, when you take a stand for right, someone will tell the people in power and control. *"But there are some Jews whom you have set over the affairs of the province of Babylon--Shadrach, Meshach and Abednego--who pay no attention to you, O king. They neither serve your gods nor worship the image of gold you have set up."* (Daniel 3:12). The same thing is true today in the church and in society. Someone will tell on you. Someone might tell big brother government that you should lose your tax exempt status because you were preaching hate speech by saying that God said, "thou shalt not" when people want the freedom to do whatever feels good to them. Some groups will threaten you with legal action for calling the name of Christ in a setting where people of other religions might hear even though they will claim free speech rights to call the name of their god.

Shadrach, Meshach and Abednego replied to the king, "O Nebuchadnezzar, we do not need to defend ourselves before you in this matter. If we are thrown into the blazing furnace, the God we serve is able to save us from it, and he will rescue us from your hand, O king. But even if he does not, we want you to know, O king, that we will not serve your gods or worship the image of gold you have set up," (Daniel 3:16-18).

Chapter 2

My God Sent an Angel

Daniel answered, "O king, live forever! My God sent his angel, and he shut the mouths of the lions. They have not hurt me, because I was found innocent in his sight. Nor have I ever done any wrong before you, O king." (Daniel 6:21,22).

Daniel was an amazing man. He, along with his Hebrew friends, had endured the worst kind of abuse and abasement. He was kidnaped, enslaved, and possibly even castrated. Yet he remained true to God and never questioned or denied God. His Hebrew companions had been tried by fire and survived to be restored and elevated by a very impressed king. Daniel had interpreted the monarch's dreams while under a death sentence and enjoyed the consequent praise and promotion from a grateful king. In fact, *Daniel so distinguished himself among the administrators and the satraps by his exceptional qualities that the king planned to set him over the whole kingdom.* (Daniel 6:3).

It is good, on the one hand, to be recognized for our competence and fidelity by those in authority over us. Who would not want the boss at work to see our good work and recommend us for a promotion? However, there are risks associated with this kind of favorable attention. Jealousy often comes to the fore with significant negative consequences. That's exactly what happened to Daniel. *The administrators and the satraps tried to find grounds for charges against Daniel in his conduct of government affairs, but they were unable to do so. They could find no corruption in him, because he was trustworthy and neither corrupt nor negligent.* (Daniel 6:4). They knew that Daniel's one weakness was his greatest strength, his fidelity to his God. *Finally these men said, "We will never find any basis for charges against this man Daniel unless it has something to do with the law of his God."* (Daniel 6:5). Is your weakness your honesty, your fidelity to God and your belief that you serve a God who sits high and looks low?

If people can't find any failing, they will invent something. This explains why the other administrators cooked up the scheme that would get Daniel thrown into the lions' den. *The royal administrators, prefects, satraps, advisers and governors have all agreed that the king should issue an edict and enforce the decree that anyone who prays to any god or man during the next thirty days, except to you, O king, shall be thrown into the lions' den.* (Daniel 6:7). Some people with authority and power develop god complexes where they see themselves as worthy of such reverence that they become gods in the eyes of their subjects. This idea is not peculiar to pagan cultures, but also is presented in the Hebrew Scriptures. *"I said, 'You are "gods", you are all sons of the Most High.' But you will die like mere men; you will fall like every other ruler."* (Psalm 82:6). To the Catholics, this god might be the Pope; to the Methodists, the bishop, to the Baptists, the pastor or head of the deacon board. Even the citizens of an atheistic, totalitarian regime make "gods" of the despotic dictator. These gods are warned that their positions and authority may give them the status of gods in the eyes of their subjects and subordinates, however, they are reminded that they *"will die like mere men."*

The greatest temptation faced by many Christians is the urge to yield to the dictates of the gods rather than follow the commands of God Almighty. Obeying the gods might lead to advancement. Offending them might mean the end of your career. We can learn an important lesson from Daniel's response to the decree. *Now when Daniel learned that the decree had been published, he went home to his upstairs room where the windows opened toward Jerusalem. Three times a day he got down on his knees and prayed, giving thanks to his God, just as we have done before.* (Daniel 6:10). The government tried to tell Daniel how to pray and to whom he should pray. He continued to do what he had always done; he honored God through daily prayer. He did not try to hide it. He did not become a closet Christian. He did not sneak in a prayer like some people do when they go out to dinner and think that someone might see them saying a prayer of thanks to God. Nor did Daniel decry the government edict.

I will not accept invitations to give the invocation or benediction at some public events because the organization has put restrictions on the prayer. They may require special language or forbid a prayer in Jesus' name. They have every right to make such requests but I refuse because I will always pray as usual without any imposed restrictions.

Daniel knew that gods--people who think they have power--always have someone who will tell, someone who is ambitious and wants to win their favor. Someone will speed-dial the king and tell him what we are doing wrong. However, if we are faithful, we, like Daniel will serve God just as we had done before. Daniel knew that the God he served was able to deliver him from the evil ones. The king had been tricked into issuing the decree in such a way that even he could not change it. He had to have Daniel thrown into the lions' den. The king had been so impressed by Daniel's God that he hoped that his God would be able to save him.

The king spent a sleepless night worrying about

Daniel and hoping that Daniel's God would come through once again. Early in the morning, he rushed to the lions' den and called out to Daniel. He wanted to know if Daniel's God had done it again. Was Daniel still alive? Many god-kings have only a vicarious knowledge of the living God. They have witnessed the power of God working in the lives of the Daniels of the world but they still don't know God for themselves. Daniel's answer showed that Daniel had a personal relationship with God. He did not serve a God about whom he had merely heard. *Daniel answered, "O king, live forever! My God sent his angel, and he shut the mouths of the lions. They have not hurt me, because I was found innocent in his sight. Nor have I ever done any wrong before you, O king."* (Daniel 6:21,22).

The king was overjoyed and greatly impressed, but he was not converted to a righteous point of view. *At the king's command, the men who had falsely accused Daniel were brought in and thrown into the lions' den, along with their wives and children. And before they reached the floor of the den, the lions overpowered them and crushed all their bones.* (Daniel 6:24). The ultimate punishment in the minds of despotic rulers in the ancient Near Eastern world was not only the death of the perpetrator, but also his wives and children so that his family name was wiped from the face of the earth.

Darius was truly impressed, but he did not really learn a lesson from his first decree. So, he issued another decree. It seems, on the surface, that he was trying to do a good thing. *"I issue a decree that in every part of my kingdom people must fear and reverence the God of Daniel. For he is the living God and he endures forever; his kingdom will not be destroyed, his dominion will never end."* (Daniel 6:20). King Darius knew that Daniel's God was an awesome God, but he did not know God for himself.

Darius believed in gods but did not have a personal relationship with the true God of the universe.

Sometimes we must experience the "lions' den". Peter explains why this may happen. *In this you greatly rejoice, though now for a little while you may have had to suffer grief in all kinds of trials. These have come so that your faith--of greater worth than gold, which perishes even though refined by fire--may be proved genuine and may result in praise, glory and honor when Jesus Christ is revealed.* (1 Peter 1:6-8).

When we are in the midst of the most difficult times in life facing the lions with sharp, gnashing teeth we need to be able to shout that, "My God sent his angel". My only visit to Las Vegas came when I was a passenger on an airplane that had a fire in the engine. I am an absolute coward who should have been terrified in that situation. But I felt a peaceful calm as the pilot made an emergency landing on the foam covered runway. I understood even then that my God sent an angel. Black ice on a darkened highway in North Carolina caused my car to go sailing off the road into the unknown. My God sent an angel as we landed softly in the snow. A dear friend of mine was in the hospital being assaulted by the intense pains of a debilitating, incurable disease. My God sent an angel, the death angel, to release her from the lions' jaws called pain and escort her to the presence of God.

Yes, sometimes the angel brings death as a sweet release from the jaws of the lions. *When the perishable has been clothed with the imperishable, and the mortal with immortality, then the saying that is written will come true: "Death has been swallowed up in victory. Where, O death, is your victory? Where, O death, is your sting?" The sting of death is sin, and the power of sin is the law.* (1 Corinthians 15:54-56). Paul goes on to thank God for the victory in

Christ that allows us to stand firm like Daniel and carry on with business as usual. *But thanks be to God! He gives us the victory through our Lord Jesus Christ. Therefore, my dear brothers, stand firm. Let nothing move you. Always give yourselves fully to the work of the Lord, because you know that your labor in the Lord is not in vain.* (1 Corinthians 15:57-58).

Even if life presents *dangers, toils and snares*, remember that God will send an angel of mercy to rescue you.

Chapter 3

The Magnificent Mystery

However, as it is written: "No eye has seen, no ear has heard, no mind has conceived what God has prepared for those who love him" but God has revealed it to us by his Spirit. The Spirit searches all things, even the deep things of God. (1 Corinthians 2:9,10).

*M*any people think that mystery means something that our minds need to figure out. A mystery to the Christian transcends our mental abilities and soars to the place where knowledge comes only from revelation by the Spirit of God. Paul explained that our intellect and common senses cannot perceive what God has prepared for those who love God. We can't figure this out. These *"deep things of God"* are available only to those who love God. Love is the key. The requirement to participate in this mystery is that we must be *like-minded, having the same love, being one in spirit and purpose.* (Philippians 2:2).

Your attitude should be the same as that of Christ Jesus. (Philippians 2:5). The Authorized Version uses the well-known expression, *Let this mind be in you, which was also in Christ Jesus.* We need to think about life in the same way that Jesus thought when he was on earth in the flesh. What was this attitude of Christ? In another place, Paul declares that we have the mind of Christ, *"For who has known the mind of the Lord that he may instruct him?" But we have the mind of Christ.* (1 Corinthians. 2:16).

It was an attitude of humility. This is saying a lot. Most of us are very interested in recognition, status, and having others defer to us. We want plaques to hang on the wall and certificates of merit. We want the highest grade and, of course, all of our children are well above average. Christ was meek and lowly. *"Who, being in very nature God, did not consider equality with God something to be grasped, but made himself nothing."* (Philippians 2:6). This is one of the most difficult and debated scriptures in the entire Bible. The Greek word for what Jesus did is *ekenosen*; it is active, not passive. This was not something that was done to Jesus. Jesus did it. He *made himself nothing.* He "emptied himself." Some theologians get nervous and uncomfortable with this translation. They argue that Jesus was always God and remained fully God throughout his incarnation. I believe that they are correct. However, God, who is sovereign, can define the godly characteristics during any phase of God's existence.

I believe that this view is neither frightening nor heretical. It is in fact the highest expression of the love of God. Jesus' love was so great that he voluntarily set aside his divine characteristics and entrusted them to the one whom he called Father. He could ask for them at any time through prayer but he could not invoke them on his own. To say that God *"gave his son"* means that all persons of the Trinity were full participants in the process of giving. Thus, Christ *"gave"* himself. He did it, in part, through this kenosis or emptying of himself.

Consider some of the characteristics of God: omnipresence, omniscience, omnipotence. Jesus, as the agent of creation in eternity past had all of these characteristics and more. Omnipresence means the ability to be everywhere at once. God is like that. But Jesus chose to take a human body, which could only be in one place at a time. He voluntarily set aside this godly characteristic when he chose to take on a human body. If he had remained omnipresent he would not have been confined to the cross since only a minute part of his being would have been nailed to that stake while he was omnipresent throughout the rest of creation.

Omniscience means all knowing or all wise. The fact is that Jesus himself said that there were some things that he did not know. Only the Father knew them. Before you throw things at me and accuse me of blasphemy consider, *No one knows about that day or hour, not even the angels in heaven, nor the Son, but only the Father.* (Mark 13:32). It seems pretty clear to me. Even the Son didn't know certain things while he was on earth in his human form.

Omnipotence means that God has all power. The triune God has and always had all power. Therefore, the pre-incarnate Christ had all power. In what ways did Jesus limit his power? He took his share of power and entrusted it to the ones he called Father and Holy Spirit.

Many of the most conservative biblical exegetes are greatly disturbed by these ideas. They take great offense at the notion that Jesus' divinity was in any way limited or restricted by his humanity. They might be surprised to know that I share with them a zealous high regard for the unmitigated divinity and sovereignty of Christ. That sovereignty, however, includes God's ability to become manifest in whatever form pleases God, including a human body that is subject to the space-time constraints that the non-incarnate God transcends.

His complete transformation to servanthood showed that the relinquishing of his highest attributes was complete. The Bible describes the incarnate Christ as *taking the very nature of a servant being made in human likeness.* (Philippians 2:7). This notion was so difficult for the apostles to grasp that Jesus had to demonstrate his status and his commandment by washing their feet. *And being found in appearance as a man, he humbled himself and became obedient to death--even death on a cross!* (Philippians 2:8).

Christmas is a wonderful holiday. I especially enjoy the time with family and friends. But Christmas without Easter would be an empty time of crass consumerism. This is why we celebrate the Resurrection Sunday called Easter. If he had not gone about his Father's business; if he had resisted the Holy Spirit that rested and remained on him; if he had not become obedient to death on a cross, we would have nothing to celebrate on Easter morning.

Therefore God exalted him to the highest place and gave him the name that is above every name, that at the name of Jesus every knee should bow, in heaven and on earth and under the earth, and every tongue confess that Jesus Christ is Lord, to the glory of God the Father. (Philippians 2:9,10). Because he was obedient to the plan that he had developed in eternity with the Father and the Holy Spirit, he was given a name above all names. That obedience came from one who limited himself to the same constraints that we experience. We cannot claim the excuse of human limitations as we cop a plea for our sinful failures. Jesus proved that the power of God transcends human limitations if we are obedient to God and empowered by the Holy Spirit.

We celebrate the resurrection of Jesus on Easter morning. Many of us have never truly understood the idea that he died for us. After all, if he kept control over all of his divine attributes, he was not truly experiencing what a real man would experience. Merely feeling physical pain, no matter how agonizing would not have been enough. Many men and women have experienced even more intense pain than that suffered by Jesus. If he had known that he could of his own volition come down off of the cross and end his agony, it would have diminished the effect of his passion. Moreover, if there had been no risk, if he had just been pretending to depend on the Father and the Holy Spirit while remaining in control of his divine attributes, he would have risked nothing but a finite measure of physical pain.

That's why I can sing with my ancestors "Sometimes it causes me to tremble" when I think about what Jesus risked. He put eternity on the line for us. If he had failed, not only would we still be lost in our sins; he would have lost eternity. Don't profane and demean the sacrifice of our savior with bunnies and eggs. Let us honor him by committing our lives to humble service. Thank him for enduring that empty feeling that lasted until his post-resurrection declaration, *"All authority in heaven and on earth has been given to me."* (Matthew 28:18). He gave it up and now he had it back. He completed his mission, reclaimed his eternally divine heritage and resumed his rightful position of authority with the Father and the Holy Spirit.

Even if you have human frailties, the Holy Spirit who abides in you can transcend your human limitations.

Chapter 4

Good News at Sunrise

Then the eleven disciples went to Galilee, to the mountain where Jesus had told them to go. When they saw him, they worshiped him; but some doubted. (Matthew 28:16-17).

Day after day every priest stands and performs his religious duties; again and again he offers the same sacrifices, which can never take away sins. But when this priest had offered for all time one sacrifice for sins, he sat down at the right hand of God. (Hebrews 10:11-12).

   Sunrise is a time of hope. The gloom of the end of the day as the sun sets is replaced by the expectancy of new possibilities. This is especially true when we consider Easter sunrise and reflect on the overwhelming joy that accompanies the thought that Jesus died and then rose again to save us from our sins and provide eternal life. That is why the initial reaction of the disciples is both surprising and disconcerting. *"When they saw him, they worshiped him; but some doubted."* (Matthew 28:17). They worshiped him because they had seen and experienced the miracles. They worshiped him because his appearance alive meant that they, too, could still hope for life. They worshiped him because they loved him and he reciprocated with a holy love. We are not surprised that they worshiped him, but why the doubt? They were looking at Jesus in the flesh. Why did they doubt?

Many Christians read the latest novel that calls the resurrection into question and they doubt. Others watch the television special on the alleged grave of Jesus and Mary and they doubt. Some read about or experience horrendous tragedies and they doubt. The first disciples remembered the terrible reality of the crucifixion that they had witnessed and they doubted. They thought about the seven last cries from the cross and they doubted. No man could have survived the intense torture experienced by Jesus. He was truly dead. They saw his lifeless body entombed in Joseph's crypt and they doubted.

The greatest source of doubt comes when something does not make sense. Jesus' words and actions did not make sense. How could he cry from the cross *"forgive them because they don't know what they are doing"* (Luke 23:34)? No wonder they doubted. The disciples knew the ancient scriptures. They went to the temple on the required days and made the sacrifices that would put them in good standing with God. They had not understood Jesus when he tried to show them that he would be the last, perfect sacrifice that would end the need for sacrifices forever. *Sacrifice and offering you did not desire, but my ears you have pierced; burnt offerings and sin offerings you did not require. Then I said, "Here I am, I have come--it is written about me in the scroll. I desire to do your will, O my God; your law is within my heart."* (Psalm 40:6-8).

They had heard Jesus when he told a man who had violated every commandment of God that he would be with him in paradise. What were they to make of this rash promise to a common criminal? How could it be that one so vile and evil could have that promise while the disciples of Jesus were cowering in doubt and fear?

Modern-day theologians argue about what Jesus meant when he told one thief on the cross, *"I tell you the truth, today you will be with me in paradise."* (Luke 23:43). Some suggest that the placement of the comma before or after "today" could change the meaning of the sentence. Contentions about such fine points are irrelevant. The important point is that Jesus said to the thief the same thing that he said to the disciples, *you will be with me.* As a favorite psalm says, *through the valley of the shadow of death, you are with me.* (Psalm 23:4). Even from the cross, Jesus was still teaching his followers life-changing lessons. The vilest criminal, despite a lifetime of evil deeds, can enter the place prepared by Jesus if he puts his trust in Him. Even more than that, John's gospel records the fact that Jesus promised his troubled disciples that he was going to prepare a place for them (John 14:1-4) so that they could be with him.

Even if we are facing the specter of the cross, the joyous message is that the old person is crucified with Christ so that the new person can rise with him to take a place he has prepared in his kingdom.

Chapter 5

Jesus Can Work It Out

From this time many of his disciples turned back and no longer followed him. (John 6:66).

Many controversies about Jesus during his earthly lifetime involved his work. Some people were so troubled by the things that he said that they *walked with him no more* (John 6:66). His ideas were dangerous *"hard sayings."* (John 6:60). But they were abstractions that could be explained away. His works, however, were observed by so many that they could not be misinterpreted or denied. They saw him heal the lame man and command him to take up his bed and walk. They witnessed the healing of the blind man who could now find his way without help. The man who was dead was now walking around singing the praises of Jesus who called him back to life. The works of Jesus could not be hidden.

Jesus' disciples were very nervous about the Master's deeds. They knew that spies were in the congregations reporting on his every action. The disciples tried to get him to be a little more discreet and cautious. But Jesus said to them, *"My Father is always at his work to this very day, and I, too, am working."* (John 5:17). Moreover, he said, *as long as it is day, we must do the work of him who sent me. Night is coming, when no one can work.* (John 9:4). Jesus was driven to do the work of the Father. He was not about to hide out to be safe and avoid his calling. Jesus is the Light of the World who brings the perpetual daylight that allows the children of God to see how to do the work that they have been given.

Jesus was a partner with his earthly stepfather, Joseph, in the carpentry trade. He was also a partner with his real Father in heaven. In fact, it was this divine union with the Father that enabled him to do the miraculous works that he did. Even the amazing words that Jesus used were given to him by the Father. *Don't you believe that I am in the Father, and that the Father is in me? The words I say to you are not just my own. Rather, it is the Father, living in me, who is doing his work. Believe me when I say that I am in the Father and the Father is in me; or at least believe on the evidence of the miracles themselves.* (John 14:10-11). The evidence was the work, the miracles that Jesus was able to perform. He didn't just talk about bringing new life. He raised people from the dead.

Then Jesus went on to make a promise that has been seriously misinterpreted by many latter-day believers. He promised the Apostles that they would be able to do even *"greater works"* (KJV) than he had done. *I tell you the truth, anyone who has faith in me will do what I have been doing. He will do even greater things than these, because I am going to the Father. And I will do whatever you ask in my name, so that the Son may bring glory to the Father. You may ask me for anything in my name, and I will do it.* (John 14:12-14).

I have often reflected on what Jesus meant by this statement. I know that he meant what he said because Jesus always told the truth and nothing but the truth. The question is what did he mean by *"greater works"* and to whom was the promise made? I suspect that no matter how hard I work, I will never raise anyone from the dead. I don't believe that I will be able to spit into some mud, rub it on someone's eyes and cause them to see. Despite all of my years of studying chemistry I do not believe that I will ever be able to turn water into wine. In other words, I don't see how I can even do the same things that Jesus did. So how in the world can I do *"greater works"* than Jesus? Could Jesus have meant greater in the sense of "more than" in the same way that ten is greater than five? Jesus was preparing to return to the Father where he would be able to help the disciples who remained on earth to do even more miracles than he had done. In addition, Jesus said that as he returned to the Father, the Holy Spirit would stand beside the disciples and empower them to do even more than Jesus had been able to do in his limited time in the flesh on earth.

Jesus not only got into trouble for the kind of work that he did. He was also criticized for when he did it. He made a habit of doing his work on the Sabbath when others would declare that it was unlawful for him to work. Those from my generation or older remember how zealous our parents were about respecting Sunday as a day when we did only the minimum amount of work required to live. Some faithful mothers even cooked Sunday dinner on Saturday night. The community heaped scorn on those who did unnecessary work or play on Sunday. Jesus understood, however, that the Sabbath was a special gift to working people, a time for them to do the work of honoring God. Before the institution of the Sabbath, poor working people had no excuse to stop working. The masters and mistresses could sit and sip mint juleps, but field workers worked in the fields until they dropped from exhaustion. Farmers like my late father-in-law had to work the farm seven days a week. But, Sunday's work was only the bare minimum essentials as they shut the main operations down to go to church. This day of rest and reverence was a divine gift. Many people who ridicule the devotion of our fathers and mothers to church have no appreciation for the historical significance of this blessed day.

Jesus asked the lame man by the pool at Bethesda if he had the will to be made whole. Being whole did not mean merely to get up and walk though that was the most important thing to the man. The real question was whether he had the will to do the work that he was asked to do, that is, to carry the mat. He knew that it would be against the law for him to carry the mat on the Sabbath Day. Standing up and walking would be an important miracle. But it would not make the man whole. A whole person does more than stand and walk. A whole person has someplace to go and has something to do. If you are not going to work, you may as well stay on the mat and beg. If you are not going to work, there is no real purpose for your healing. When God told Moses and Aaron to tell Pharaoh to let the Hebrews go it was so that they could worship God on the mountain. There was a sacred purpose for their liberation. There was a divine purpose for releasing the lame man from bondage. Jesus put him to work carrying his mat as a witness to the world about the power of Jesus to heal and to set free.

Society did indeed confront the lame man as he proudly did the work that Jesus gave him to do. They chided him that he surely knew that this was the Sabbath and that he was breaking the law by carrying his mat. His answer was the only valid answer that one can give when the cynics and the naysayers challenge what we are doing in the church. "I am doing what the man who set me free told me to do."

The man did not know Jesus' name, yet he knew Jesus and he believed that Jesus could work it out. Jesus can work out our confusion, our uncertainty, and our doubts. Jesus can work out our fear of our detractors. Jesus can work it out even when our family and loved ones question our will and determination.

Think about the kind of work that God requires. *Then they asked him, "What must we do to do the works God requires?"* (John 6:28). *Jesus answered, "The work of God is this: to believe in the one he has sent,"* (John 6:29). The job description for the disciples of Christ is to simply believe. Just believe in Jesus and Jesus will work it out.

Critics outside of the church will ask loudly, "What kind of work are you people doing inside of that church?" Any answer you give will never be satisfactory. It will never be enough. If you say that we have a food pantry where we feed and clothe the hungry and the needy, they will reply that you ought to be doing more. If you say that we visit the sick their retort will be that you don't visit enough. If you say that we sent money to help the victims of disasters such as Katrina, they will reply that you haven't made any difference to those unfortunate people. Next time, give the answer that will really mess with their mind, "Our work is to believe in Jesus Christ, the Son of God." We just believe Jesus.

Even if our work seems overwhelming and daunting, Jesus can work it out if you *commit to the LORD whatever you do, and your plans will succeed.* (Proverbs16:3). Jesus is the one who could say from the cross, *"It is finished!"* Jesus is the one who could pray, *I have brought you glory on earth by completing the work you gave me to do.* (John 17:4).

Chapter 6

The Full Gospel

Now, brothers, I want to remind you of the gospel I preached to you, which you received and on which you have taken your stand. By this gospel you are saved, if you hold firmly to the word I preached to you. Otherwise, you have believed in vain. (1 Corinthians 15:1-2).

There are some churches today that claim to be "full gospel" churches. This declaration does not bother me even when the claimant says it with a superior smirk or sneer. Those who are reading this chapter should know that while we will not change our name, I pastor a full gospel church. Being anything else would mean that we are preaching a partial or incomplete gospel. Paul addressed this question during the first century in his first extant letter to the church at Corinth. *Now, brothers, I want to remind you of the gospel I preached to you, which you received and on which you have taken your stand.* (1 Corinthians 15:1).

There were so many new things in Paul's day including so-called new gospels. Some preachers claimed to have special knowledge of God that only they could reveal. Others offered unusual ecstatic experiences and special revelations of the divine. That's why Paul felt the need to remind them of the gospel that he preached and that they had received. He reminded them as they were seduced by other religious teachings that *by this gospel you are saved, if you hold firmly to the word I preached to you. Otherwise, you have believed in vain.* (1 Corinthians 15:2). Paul tells them that if they don't hold on to what they have heard from him they will have believed in vain. What they already have is the gospel by which they were saved and through which they have made their stand.

The "full gospel" is so simple that it only contains three parts: (1) Christ died for our sins; (2) He was buried; (3) He rose again on the third day. The first part seems to be easy. In fact we say it so often that it sounds trite and obvious. Christ died. He was not asleep. He was not in a coma. He was completely, totally and physically, dead. Moreover, this death had a specific purpose. Many of us suffer great spiritual agony as we reflect on the apparently senseless death of so many of our young people. They died for no purpose. Christ died for our sins. This means that Christ died as a direct result of our sinful actions and Christ died to atone for our sinful behavior. Our sin was not necessarily our voice crying *"crucify him!"* Our sin was our silence. Our sin was our self-imposed blindness. Our sin was our lack of action. Our sin was our failure to love. Christ died for our sins.

He was buried. Why did Paul include this in the list? Burial usually follows death except for one who was cursed to die on a tree by crucifixion. Part of the punishment was that the family had to see the body thrown into the garbage dump called Gehenna where the animals and the maggots would slowly consume the body. Decay follows burial. Peter thought that the burial was important enough that he included it in his great post-Pentecostal sermon. *Because you will not abandon me to the grave, nor will you let your Holy One see decay. You have made known to me the paths of life; you will fill me with joy in your presence. Brothers, I can tell you confidently that the patriarch David died and was buried, and his tomb is here to this day. But he was a prophet and knew that God had promised him on oath that he would place one of his descendants on his throne.* (Acts 2:27-30).

He rose again on the third day. This is a necessary part of Christianity. *Seeing what was ahead, he spoke of the resurrection of the Christ, that he was not abandoned to the grave, nor did his body see decay.* (Acts 2:31). There is no option here. You can't say that it doesn't matter. *God has raised this Jesus to life, and we are all witnesses of the fact.* (Acts 2:32). This completes the entire process. *Brothers, we do not want you to be ignorant about those who fall asleep, or to grieve like the rest of men, who have no hope. We believe that Jesus died and rose again and so we believe that God will bring with Jesus those who have fallen asleep in him.* (1 Thessalonians 4:13-14). *Therefore encourage one another and build each other up, just as in fact you are doing.* (1 Thessalonians 5:11).

Even if others challenge your faith, be assured that this is the full gospel. Nothing can be added to it and nothing taken away. Take away any part and you don't have the gospel. Add anything to it as being required for salvation and you diminish its power.

Chapter 7

Where Did The Weeds Come From?

Jesus told them another parable: "The kingdom of heaven is like a man who sowed good seed in his field. But while everyone was sleeping, his enemy came and sowed weeds among the wheat, and went away. When the wheat sprouted and formed heads, then the weeds also appeared. "The owner's servants came to him and said, 'Sir, didn't you sow good seed in your field? Where then did the weeds come from?' " 'An enemy did this,' he replied. "The servants asked him, 'Do you want us to go and pull them up?' 'No,' he answered, 'because while you are pulling the weeds, you may root up the wheat with them. Let both grow together until the harvest. At that time I will tell the harvesters: First collect the weeds and tie them in bundles to be burned; then gather the wheat and bring it into my barn.' " (Matthew 13:24-30).

Recently, I attended the funeral of a brother beloved in the ministry. The eight-hour round trip was made even more difficult by the tragic circumstances of his brutal murder and the remaining unsolved and unresolved mysteries surrounding his sudden death. The journey and funeral service were so emotionally draining that later that night, I could not eat the meal and join the festivities for the retirement of our esteemed bishop. I prayed for the pastor who had the unenviable task of preaching to the gathered family that included the fallen brother's two beautiful and intelligent young daughters, one of whom read a very touching poetic tribute to their father. The pastor's eulogy was stunning in its elegance, simplicity, and spiritual power. His title, *An Enemy Has Done This*, serves as the inspiration for this chapter.

Now and then Jesus would seize the opportunity to teach his disciples. These periodic explanations were necessary because the clueless disciples thought they knew and understood the mysteries of heaven and, of course, got it wrong. Jesus told a parable that had the purpose of helping his disciples to understand the kingdom of heaven. *Jesus told them another parable: "The kingdom of heaven is like a man who sowed good seed in his field. But while everyone was sleeping his enemy came and sowed weeds among the wheat, and went away."* (Matthew 13:24-25).

Eventually, the crop developed and it was immediately apparent that there was a problem. *"The owner's servants came to him and said, 'Sir, didn't you sow good seed in your field? Where then did the weeds come from?"* (Matthew 13:27). That's the question that we are asking today about our society. Where did the weeds come from? The Bible tells us that God's creative work was good. The original garden was good. It was filled with wonderful things to behold and to eat. There were no weeds. Where did the weeds come from? The answer was the same in the beginning as it was in Jesus' parable — an enemy has done this. Jesus explained to his puzzled disciples that the enemy was the devil. God's actions are always good. When bad things happen you can be assured, an enemy has done this.

We are still left to wonder why. I have thought about this question often in over thirty-nine years in the ministry. Most of us in our rare honest moments would admit that we think we know what we would do if we had God's power. We are afraid to say "If I were God…"

though we think it. Instead, we intone "If I had the power, I would..." We would know how to handle the bad guys and we would surely intervene to prevent evil people from carrying out their dastardly deeds. This all leads to the ultimate question of the skeptical believer. Why does God permit the bad actors to go unchecked? There is a hint of an answer in Romans. *Furthermore, since they did not think it worthwhile to retain the knowledge of God, he gave them over to a depraved mind, to do what ought not to be done.* (Romans 1:28). He gave them over. God did not prevent evil people from becoming what they were determined to be. He gave them over. God did not will it, but God did permit them to have the desires of their heart to do evil instead of good.

Has God ever had to give you over to a depraved [reprobate, KJV] mind? God commands us to love. Have you ever been so determined to hate that God gave you over to wallow in the filth of your hatred? God demands sexual purity and fidelity. Have you ever become so consumed by your lusts that you declare that you were born this way so that you can't help yourself? God demands, truth, honesty and integrity. Do you find yourself stretching the truth and ignoring the wrongs that should be made right? Do you insist on abusing your body in illegal or unsafe ways and perverting your mind with visual and audible filth? God may have given you over to a depraved mind. The good news is that even then God has not given up on you. It's not too late for you to have a change of mind. *Your attitude* [mind, KJV] *should be the same as that of Christ Jesus.* (Philippians 2:5).

As we reflect on the legacy of assassinated leaders we realize that an enemy has done this because so many people were given over to the reprobate and depraved minds that propagate the festering sores of prejudice and injustice. The great sin of my beloved country is not only that she continues to practice pervasive and devastating racism but the absolute refusal to repent and honor the God who is *no respecter of persons*. The raucous debate about sound bites from the sermon of a former pastor to a presidential candidate serves the positive role of reminding us that there are those growing like weeds among us who have been given up to depraved minds that cannot stand prophetic convicting preaching. I don't defend that pastor's choice of words. He doesn't need my defense. I applaud his boldness that convicts the timid and tentative preachers who have let the weeds choke the life out of the wheat.

When Jesus has the parable's servants ask the question *"Where did the weeds come from?"* he might have been thinking of the coming meal when the enemy would enter Judas and cause him to betray the Master. We need to think about this when we celebrate the special meal shared by Jesus and his close disciples. We need not enter the debate along with the theologians about exactly when Judas left to do his dirt. Suffice it to say that he was on the scene during the time of the meal. *Then Jesus replied, "Have I not chosen you, the Twelve? Yet one of you is a devil!" (He meant Judas, the son of Simon Iscariot, who, though one of the Twelve, was later to betray him.)* (John 6:70-71). Jesus said that Judas was a devil, the enemy himself. Yet Jesus allowed this weed to grow among the wheat and did not cut him down.

The time will come when God will subdue the enemy. Satan will be cast down. The demise of the devil means that the deadly consequences of his influence will also end. *Then the end will come, when he hands over the kingdom to God the Father after he has destroyed all dominion, authority and power. For he must reign until he has put all his*

enemies under his feet. The last enemy to be destroyed is death.
(1 Corinthians 15:24-26).

Even if the unimaginable happens, we will have eternal
life with the Savior who allowed the weeds to grow until
the wheat was tall enough to tower over them so that the
weeds could be removed and the wheat harvested.

Chapter 8

When You Wish You Had Never Been Born

When evening came, Jesus arrived with the Twelve. While they were reclining at the table eating, he said, "I tell you the truth, one of you will betray me--one who is eating with me." They were saddened, and one by one they said to him, "Surely not I?" "It is one of the Twelve," he replied, "one who dips bread into the bowl with me. The Son of Man will go just as it is written about him. But woe to that man who betrays the Son of Man! It would be better for him if he had not been born." (Mark 14:17-21).

Judas reached a point in his life when the prediction of Jesus came true. He truly wished that he had never been born. It wasn't just his actions that led him to that point. It was the realization that he could not undo his actions after re-thinking his plan. Sometimes when you are having a very bad day, you might cry out in anguish, "I wish I had never been born!" When you lash out in anger at an adversary against whom you intend to take vengeance you might exclaim, "You will regret the day that you were born!" We probably don't feel very religious or Spirit-filled during those times but they are reminiscent of words spoken by Jesus himself on that last arduous journey to Golgotha.

Jesus was carrying the cross on his way to Calvary to die for our sins. There were many people who followed him and others who stood along the side of the road looking on. Luke points out that a *large number of people followed him, including women who mourned and wailed for him.* (Luke 23:27). Jesus called the women who mourned and wailed for him the Daughters of Jerusalem. They might have included women who were hired by families to mourn at funerals and before and during impending death due to execution. Mourning would have been their job. It was to them that Jesus said, *do not weep for me; weep for yourselves and for your children.* (Luke 23:28). He seemed to be saying that if they can do this to someone who is innocent of any wrongdoing then imagine what is going to happen to you who are declared guilty of transgressions against the state or others in power. Though the exact meaning is still debated by scholars, this may be the implication of the cryptic saying, *For if men do these things when the tree is green, what will happen when it is dry?* (Luke 23:31). Remember how your mother used to say when you complained about ill treatment, "If they crucified the Lord, imagine what they will do to you?" I don't know who "they" are in your life but if you have ever been accused and persecuted then you understand what Jesus was saying to the women along the road on that day. Their pain would be so great that they would regret the day they were born.

The centurion, the professional military officer who was looking with secular eyes, saw Jesus as *a righteous man* suffering unjustly. He was a non-Jew and non-believer in Christ. He was jaded from having witnessed so many crucifixions. He knew the pattern. He knew the drill. He had become immune to the cries of pain and agony. But there was something different about Jesus. Matthew suggests that he realized even more than that; he perceived that Jesus was truly divine.

When the centurion and those who were with him guarding Jesus saw the earthquake and all that had happened, they were terrified, and exclaimed, "Surely he was the Son of God!" (Matthew 27:54).

The other spectators who did not know Jesus but who had come to witness this show, made some gestures and left. The curiosity seekers went away. Those looking for a show realized that the show was almost over. They left. Those who wanted him to die went away because they realized that he was practically dead. The discouraged and despondent went away. *But all those who knew him including the women who had followed him from Galilee, stood at a distance watching these things.* (Luke 23:49). One can visualize them standing at a distance feeling helpless but refusing to leave the Master. We must note that this drama orchestrated and played out by men was also witnessed by the women who had followed him all the way from Galilee and would not leave him now.

Part of the punishment of this cruel crucifixion process was that family and friends had to witness the humiliation and suffer vicariously with their condemned loved one. This was no dignified way to die — stripped completely naked, exposed to gazing eyes, whipped, teeth knocked out and the final indignity of being forced to carry the implement of death the final dreadful steps to where it was planted in the ground so that the victim could be lifted up to be put on embarrassing display.

But that's not all. The final abuse was verbal as indicated by Mark. *Those who passed by hurled insults at him, shaking their heads and saying, "So! You who are going to destroy the temple and build it in three days, come down from the cross and save yourself!" In the same way the chief priests and the teachers of the law mocked him among themselves. "He saved others," they said, "but he can't save himself!! Let this Christ, this King of Israel, come down now from the cross, that we may see and believe." Those crucified with him also heaped insults on him.* (Mark 15:29-32). This is an interesting scripture because it shows again the crabs in the barrel syndrome. These thieves are in the same sad predicament as Jesus, yet they *also heaped insults on him.*

Recently, a well-known talk show host spoke about the President of the United States using the following words: "I hope he fails!" He elaborated and repeated the statement lest anyone misunderstand what he was saying. This lack of patriotism is so vile and irrational that it is hard to believe. It is akin to a passenger boarding an airplane where the captain was an unpopular pilot and declaring, "I hope he fails to fly this plane safely because I don't like him or his policies." I don't know about you, but the pilot of a plane on which I am flying is my best friend regardless of his or her race, gender, religion, sexual preference, color or national origin. I hope that he or she succeeds.

The kind of racism expressed by the talk show host is so asinine that it defies belief. However, witnesses in the church who are honored veterans of World War II explained that our country has long shown this kind of racist, reactionary insanity. Three of our distinguished veterans testified that black soldiers were required to do guard duty only a few hundred yards from the heavily armed enemy while they were armed only with a club or their bare hands. This ridiculous practice only changed when the white officers realized that they could not afford for the black soldiers on guard duty to fail.

These same black soldiers returned home to find that former enemy combatants who had killed American soldiers were welcomed to sit down and eat in a restaurant that was closed to the African American war heroes who risked their lives for this country. This is all very difficult to understand but we must remember that Thomas Jefferson was able to write "We hold these truths to be self-evident..." at the same time that he owned over one hundred human beings.

I wasn't a great fan of President Bush, but I assure you I never wanted him to fail. He was my President and his failure would mean that terrorists succeeded. His failure would have meant that the economy would go into the tank. His failure would mean that millions of jobs and homes would be lost. His failure would mean that thousands of brave defenders of freedom would die in the defense of his policies. I rejoice in his successes and bemoan his failures. And I pray now for the success of our new president. I hope, with millions of other loyal citizens of the United States and concerned residents of the world that he does not fail.

Though completely innocent, Jesus was unfairly crucified by those who wanted him to fail. This might be why he spoke about the green tree and the dry tree and implied that the women who were barren were blessed compared to those who gave birth to children who had to live in such a corrupt generation.

The good news is that Jesus did not fail! He was crucified like a common criminal. He seemed to be the most colossal failure. The forces of evil appeared to have triumphed. But, on the third day he rose again from the dead and re-claimed all of the power that he had from eternity past.

Even if life seems so rough that you wish that you had never been born, be glad that you were born and born again through resurrection with Christ.

Chapter 9

Power Play

One of those days Jesus went out to a mountainside to pray, and spent the night praying to God. (Luke 6:12).

Near the beginning of Jesus' ministry he was still wrestling with the nature of his call. He had no doubt that he was anointed by God. He was so sure of this that he declared in his hometown synagogue that the ancient messianic prophesies were written about him. (Luke 4:16-21; Isaiah 61:1-2). Jesus had many disciples but he knew that he still needed to put his leadership team together. So, he spent the night on a mountainside praying to God for guidance. This is a tremendous example for those of us who are Christian. We often go charging off to do what we have decided to do and then pray that God will bless our efforts. We should first go up to the mountain and pray that the Holy Spirit would reveal the will of God to us. Don't buy a house and then ask God to bless it. Seek God's blessing first and then act if God commands. Don't choose a spouse and then ask God to bless the union. Ask God to send the spouse chosen by God. I was once accused by some church officers of being indecisive and taking too long to make a critical decision. I explained to the skeptical officials that God had not yet revealed the answer. I assured them that as soon as I heard from God I would make my decision.

When morning came, he called his disciples to him and chose twelve of them, whom he also designated apostles: (Luke

6:13). It was only when morning came after a night of intense prayer that Jesus called all of his disciples to him. We don't know how many disciples were there but there appear to have been many followers who had made the journey to the mountainside. *Simon (whom he named Peter), his brother Andrew, James, John, Philip, Bartholomew, Matthew, Thomas, James son of Alphaeus, Simon who was called the Zealot, Judas son of James, and Judas Iscariot, who became a traitor.* (Luke 6:14-15).

These were businessmen, tax collectors and even militant revolutionaries—a strange combination of backgrounds and experiences. Or at least it might seem strange to us but it was just the right mix in the Master's eyes. They were his cabinet, his official board, the leaders. They were the ones he would entrust to go out and make new disciples. He started his earthly ministry at the site of this mountain with these men who understood the two mountains that demand our attention. They knew how to make money and they knew how to gain power.

He took his apostles with him and found a place on the side of the mountain that was level. Some scholars believe that he went all the way down into the valley, but it may be that he found a level place in the midst of the mountain so that they were still in a high place. *He went down with them and stood on a level place. A large crowd of his disciples was there and a great number of people from all over Judea, from Jerusalem, and from the coast of Tyre and Sidon, who had come to hear him and to be healed of their diseases. Those troubled by evil spirits were cured, and the people all tried to touch him, because power was coming from him and healing them all.* (Luke 6:17-19). A crowd of other followers (disciples) was waiting for him along with the curiosity seekers, the spies, the sick and the troubled all seeking to touch him and receive a portion of his power.

Then Jesus began to preach his first sermon to his newly formed organization. *Looking at his disciples, he said: Blessed are you who are poor, for yours is the kingdom of God. Blessed are you who hunger now, for you will be satisfied. Blessed are you who weep now, for you will laugh. Blessed are you when men hate you, when they exclude you and insult you and reject your name as evil, because of the Son of Man. Rejoice in that day and leap for joy, because great is your reward in heaven. For that is how their fathers treated the prophets.* (Luke 6:20-23).

This is not a message that would have been well received by the Apostles. What a ridiculous idea, *"Blessed are you who are poor..."* Poor people don't have any money. The apostles were men who had money. Maybe that's why the scripture points out that Jesus was *"looking at his disciples"* when he preached this sermon. Jesus didn't make it any better as he continued, *"blessed are you who weep"* and *"blessed are you who hunger now."* These were not weak men who would ever cry and they always had enough food. I am sure that Jesus didn't get one "Amen" when he said *"Blessed are you when men hate you, when they exclude you and insult you and reject your name as evil, because of the Son of Man."* These were men who stood on the twin mountains of money and power. No one would dare hate them, exclude them or insult them. So they left this mountain and began the three-year crusade to proclaim that the kingdom of God was at hand.

If we keep this inaugural experience in the back of our minds, we might begin to understand some of the more cryptic sayings and actions of Jesus. The apostles regarded themselves as strong, macho men. Yet they showed behaviors that reflected the stereotypes that were often associated with women. They liked to sit around the table and gossip about Jesus behind his back and they often argued about who was going to have power and who would control the money. Two scriptures graphically illustrate this. The first is recorded in the ninth chapter of Mark: *"Teacher," said John, "we saw a man driving out demons in your name and we told him to stop, because he was not one of us." "Do not stop him," Jesus said. "No one who does a miracle in my name can in the next moment say anything bad about me"*, (Mark 9:38-39).

This scripture shows Jesus trying to teach his disciples about the mountain called power. They were arguing about who was the greatest and they told a man to stop driving out demons in the name of Jesus because the man was not one of them. He was not ordained by them. It was about them. He did not have their permission to do this work in the name of Jesus.

The second scripture, about money, re-visits a woman who we have met many times before. *While he was in Bethany, reclining at the table in the home of a man known as Simon the Leper, a woman came with an alabaster jar of very expensive perfume, made of pure nard. She broke the jar and poured the perfume on his head. Some of those present were saying indignantly to one another, "Why this waste of perfume? It could have been sold for more than a year's wages and the money given to the poor." And they rebuked her harshly. "Leave her alone," said Jesus. "Why are you bothering her? She has done a beautiful thing to me. The poor you will always have with you, and you can help them any time you want. But you will not always have me. She did what she could. She poured perfume on my body beforehand to prepare for my burial." *(Mark 14:3-8). This seems at first glance to be a criticism of the woman, but it is really a dig at Jesus about ego and money. Notice that the disciples were still gossiping. *Some of those present were saying indignantly to one another, "Why this waste of perfume?"* (Mark 14:4). They were in the presence of the master but talking among themselves about the waste of a resource that could have brought them money. Keep in mind that this "wasted" perfume was wasted in the worship of Jesus. They were saying to Jesus that instead of worshiping him, she could have sold the perfume and given the money to help the poor. They knew that they had Jesus now. What possible response could he have to that? They had forgotten that in his first mountaintop sermon, Jesus had preached, *"Blessed are the poor."*

Even at the last supper they were still thinking about the two mountains of money and power: *"What you are about to do, do quickly," Jesus told him, but no one at the meal understood why Jesus said this to him. Since Judas had charge of the money, some thought Jesus was telling him to buy what was needed for the Feast, or to give something to the poor. As soon as Judas had taken the bread, he went out. And it was night.* (John 13:27-30). If the disciples had understood they might have tried to dissuade Jesus' betrayer from his evil plan.

Well, this journey started on a mountain and it ended on a mountain: *Then the eleven disciples went to Galilee, to the mountain where Jesus had told them to go.* (Matthew 28:16). They had witnessed the power of God to resurrect their Lord. They had seen the miracles for themselves. They had also seen Jesus redefine power and shatter egos. They had heard him dismiss the importance of earthly riches while promising riches in glory. They were reluctant to let go of their worldly ideas and embrace Jesus' new idea of the kingdom. They must have been reassured despite their doubts as they heard him declare that all authority was given to him and that he would always be with them.

Even if we admit to transient doubts, we have the assurance that an all-powerful Jesus is with us to the very end.

Chapter 10

What's the Point?

The words of the Teacher, son of David, king in Jerusalem: "Meaningless! Meaningless!" says the Teacher. "Utterly meaningless! Everything is meaningless." What does man gain from all his labor at which he toils under the sun? (Eccles. 1:1-3).

Solomon must have written this scripture during a holiday season. So many people were depressed and feeling very low during that time. The Authorized Version says that everything is *"vanity."* NIV makes it very plain, *"Utterly meaningless! Everything is meaningless."* Solomon goes further to question why we even go to work. *What does man gain from all his labor at which he toils under the sun?* Some people who work for employers in certain parts of the United States can relate. Some scholars are troubled by these words and the attitude that they project. They try to rationalize and explain away Solomon's negative, fatalistic attitude.

Many people wait until the end of the year to look back and do an assessment of the year. They, like Solomon, ask what it all means and often conclude that it means nothing. The optimistic New Year's resolutions have given way to the grim realities of missed opportunities and unmet goals. Do you focus on what you did not accomplish? Some people set a goal on January 1 to lose fifteen pounds. They gained ten. Others resolved on January 1 to save money yet ended up deeper in debt. I heard many students say that they studied and still failed the test. But, I can truly say with David in Psalm 37, *"I have never seen the righteous forsaken."* We need to be reminded of this when we should be counting our blessings but so often list and catalogue all of our struggles and setbacks.

Jacob gives the prototypical example of end-time pessimism when he says, *"You have deprived me of my children. Joseph is no more and Simeon is no more, and now you want to take Benjamin. Everything is against me!"* (Genesis 42:36). If you recall the story, you know that Jacob had several good reasons to complain. He thought his favorite son Joseph was dead, a famine had overtaken his land so that his people were in danger of starvation, the Egyptian governor had kept his son Simeon as a hostage when they went to Egypt to make arrangements for desperately needed food and the final straw, the governor had demanded that his youngest son Benjamin be brought to Egypt. No wonder he cried out *"Everything is against me!"*

Did you write your Jacob's list on the last Sunday of the year? The children have strayed from the church and the family; the finance company is hounding me; the boss is talking about cutbacks and layoffs; they want to cut my retirement benefits; my spouse has lost that loving feeling…"Everything is against me!" But even Jacob's son, Joseph, was able to testify, *You intended to harm me, but God intended it for good to accomplish what is now being done, the saving of many lives.* (Genesis 50:20).

Joseph saw the hand of God working good even in the most trying and difficult circumstances. Human beings may have evil intentions, but God works with those who love God to carry them through the times of trouble. Remember Paul's words in Romans, *and we know that in all things God works for the good of those who*

love him, who have been called according to his purpose.
(Romans 8:28).

Your Jacob list is nothing more than an excuse for
failure. God wants you to look for reasons for success.
Your last action of the old year ought to be to destroy
your Jacob list. Tear it up, burn it, cut it to pieces. It's
your choice. But, get rid of the list of problems and
excuses and declare to the waiting world that *I can do
everything through him who gives me strength.* (Philippians
4:13). In fact, Paul declares, that's the secret of
contentment in any and all circumstances!

Chapter 13 of Luke tells us that Jesus was
speaking with his disciples one day when they asked him
about a disaster that had come upon some innocent
people. Pilate had killed some Galileans who apparently
were trying to prepare animals for sacrifices in the
temple. In other words, these were religious folk
engaged in the prescribed methods of worshiping God
and that heathen Pilate had them killed. Pilate mingled
human blood with the blood of sacrificial animals. There
is no indication that they asked Jesus a question. They
simply threw this difficult situation in his face and
awaited his reaction. The distraught looks on their faces
would ask the question that their lips don't speak, "How
do you explain that, Jesus?" Jesus answered the
unspoken question with the unequivocal assertion that
these Galileans were not more sinful than other
Galileans. But, he said, unless you repent you also shall
perish. Not at the hands of Pilate. Not in a tsunami or
hurricane. These did not die in these incidents because of
some greater sin but you will perish because of your sin
if you don't repent.

Many people start well at the beginning of their
Christian walk. They have the best intentions,
motivation, and high energy. At the end of the year,

some people are missing. They didn't hang in there for the whole journey. Some people who decide that all is meaningless give up and stop trying to do the right thing. A disciple of Paul named Demas was an example. Demas started well. He was called a *"fellow worker"* with Mark and Luke.

Paul tells Timothy from prison that he needs for him to come to him very soon. Everyone but Luke had abandoned him. Some left to serve in other areas of ministry. He told Timothy why Demas left and where he went: *Demas, because he loved this world, has deserted me and has gone to Thessalonica.* (2 Timothy 4:10). I wonder what it means to love this world. Isn't that a good thing? After all, was it not because God loved the world that the plan for our salvation was put in place? Demas, though, loved the world more than he loved the work of God.

I have heard parishioners say that they left one church and went to another because they were not being fed. They were apparently seeking a kind of spiritual nourishment that they could not find at the first church. It was always my suspicion, however, that their ego was malnourished. Demas loved the world. Could it be the acclaim of the world? Could it be the recognition of the world? Demas' name was second in the list of those bringing greetings behind Luke. He must have been a significant part of the ministry. Did he leave because he was tired of being number two and playing second fiddle? Was he fed up with trying to persuade Paul about the direction that the ministry should take?

I have been in the second position several times. I was an assistant pastor, an assistant director, an assistant dean and a vice-president. I am a witness that being in second place can be very frustrating. One has a great view in second place that allows one to see clearly what the idiot at the top cannot fathom.

Could it even be that he left because of the material resources and riches of the world? I am sure that Paul could earn much more as a tent maker than he received as a preacher of the gospel. Did he leave because of the danger? Paul was in prison because of his beliefs and actions. Maybe Demas decided that there was safety in the enclaves of the world compared to the dungeons awaiting those who proclaimed that Christ was alive. What's the point in depriving oneself of physical pleasure and the comforts of the world if it all has no meaning? Did Demas become an early existentialist who could not see the point? Did Demas leave Paul because he decided with the writer of Ecclesiastes that it's all meaningless? What's the point of enduring dangers, toils and snares when everything is meaningless?

We know that there is hope because after complaining about Demas, Paul told Timothy to go and find Mark and bring him because he was very helpful to him. Mark is described here as "helpful" but had been accused of failing to complete the course on an earlier journey. At the end, we realize that God gives us another chance to complete the course. And that's the point!

Even if it seems that everything is against you and life is meaningless, be reminded that God intends it for good.

Chapter 11

Anything Good

The next day Jesus decided to leave for Galilee. Finding Philip, he said to him, "Follow me." Philip, like Andrew and Peter, was from the town of Bethsaida. Philip found Nathanael and told him, "We have found the one Moses wrote about in the Law, and about whom the prophets also wrote--Jesus of Nazareth, the son of Joseph."

"Nazareth! Can anything good come from there?" Nathanael *asked. "Come and see," said Philip.* (John 1:43-46).

The incident that demands our attention in this chapter happened while Jesus was in the process of calling his disciples. He had already found Andrew and Peter. He then called Philip, who, like Peter and Andrew, was from Bethsaida, and said to him, "Follow me." A national magazine recently published an article listing the best and worst cities in the United States. As an adopted Daytonian, I bristle at the magazine's declaration that Dayton is among the worst and the dying. The foreclosure rate, unemployment, crime and struggling school system were all cited as reasons for this somber assertion. Dayton has its problems — serious problems — but it is far from dead. However, once the reputation of a city is made, most people will accept the prejudicial stereotype before they will consider any encouraging facts.

Nazareth had the same issues in Jesus' day. The world did not think much of Nazareth and Nazarenes did not think much of themselves. Nathanael's cynical question reflects the prejudicial reaction of a man who believes in stereotypes and gossip. Many of us know the sting of prejudicial responses based on race, gender, national origin, color, hair texture, state or city. Nazareth was not a town with a bad reputation. In fact, it probably was considered a nice small town in which to raise a family. Its biggest sin was not what it was. It was what it was not. It was not an exciting and glamorous place. Mark tells the story of Jesus' return to his hometown to a less than stellar reception. *Jesus left there and went to his hometown, accompanied by his disciples. When the Sabbath came, he began to teach in the synagogue, and many who heard him were amazed. "Where did this man get these things?" they asked. "What's this wisdom that has been given him, that he even does miracles! Isn't this the carpenter? Isn't this Mary's son and the brother of James, Joseph, Judas and Simon? Aren't his sisters here with us?" And they took offense at him. Jesus said to them, "Only in his hometown, among his relatives and in his own house is a prophet without honor."* (Mark 6:1-4).

We preachers often avoid verse 5 of this scripture. It describes something that God incarnate could not do. *"He could not do any miracles there, except lay his hands on a few sick people and heal them. And he was amazed at their lack of faith."* (Mark 6:5). This was a time when the historical, earthly Jesus was prevented from doing the very thing that God the Father had sent him to do because of the lack of faith of the people. Could it be that it wasn't the city that caused Nathanael's incredulous reaction to Philip? Had he heard about the cynicism and lack of faith of the people? Was he wondering whether such people could possibly produce the greatest spiritual leader of all time?

We who are Christians need to reflect on the fact that even Jesus could not help some people in certain places. Are you *"there"* in that place where even Jesus cannot do any miracles except heal a few sick people? Jesus wanted to do great things "there." Jesus wanted to do mighty works "there." All he required of those who were "there" was that they had to believe.

I have on occasion reacted from my pulpit about people who carry out certain kinds of negative activities that do not honor God in the church. Some people think that I may be over-reacting. I don't think so. Jesus violently cleared the temple of people who were doing things that dishonored God and made the house of worship a place where secular things occurred that did not respect God. He did it because he knew that the church was supposed to be a *house of prayer for all people.* He knew that God the Father had promised Solomon that if the people behaved in the proper way, then God would respond to the prayers lifted up in the House of Prayer. God would *"hear from heaven"* and give the blessing of healing. Jesus had the power to do great things but he could do no mighty works "there" because the people had not done what God required.

Even if you are from "there", remember that the greatest gift ever given to human beings came from a small town with no claim to fame.

Chapter 12

Good Manna Gone Bad

When the dew was gone, thin flakes like frost on the ground appeared on the desert floor. When the Israelites saw it, they said to each other, "What is it?" For they did not know what it was. Moses said to them, "It is the bread the LORD has given you to eat. This is what the LORD has commanded: 'Each one is to gather as much as he needs. Take an omer for each person you have in your tent.' " The Israelites did as they were told; some gathered much, some little. And when they measured it by the omer, he who gathered much did not have too much, and he who gathered little did not have too little. Each one gathered as much as he needed. Then Moses said to them, "No one is to keep any of it until morning." However, some of them paid no attention to Moses; they kept part of it until morning, but it was full of maggots and began to smell. So Moses was angry with them. (Exodus 16:14-20).

The Garden of Eden was good. The problem came when the man and woman disobeyed God's rules. It was then that paradise was lost. The story reminds us that God supplies all the needs of the people who put their full trust in God. Exodus 16 records the strange tale of good manna gone bad. The manna given by God was good if it was gathered and eaten according to God's rules. The problem wasn't God's provision which was very good. The problem was the human response to God's goodness. The provisions were given at a time when the Israelites were in the wilderness, a place and time between slavery and the freedom of the Promised Land.

God provided for the grumbling fugitives in the wilderness but they didn't even recognize what God was doing. *When the Israelites saw it, they said to each other, "What is it?" For they did not know what it was.* (Exodus 16:15a). How many times in our lives have we been staring at a gift from God while wondering what it was? Sometimes the gift comes in a strange form or an unusual place or at an unexpected time. *Moses said to them, "It is the bread the LORD has given you to eat."* (Exodus 16:15b). This is bread from heaven given by God.

God gave specific instructions about what to do with the bread that had been provided. The instructions were good. As long as they followed God's instructions, everything was all right. *This is what the LORD has commanded: 'Each one is to gather as much as he needs. Take an omer for each person you have in your tent.' The Israelites did as they were told; some gathered much, some little. And when they measured it by the omer, he who gathered much did not have too much, and he who gathered little did not have too little. Each one gathered as much as he needed.* (Exodus 16:16-18).

This was something new for Moses. Most of the people did what they were told so that everyone had as much as needed until Moses added one more instruction: *Then Moses said to them, "No one is to keep any of it until morning."* (Exodus 16:19). This was simple enough. It was the same commandment our mothers and grandmothers used to give us. "Get as much food as you want but eat all you get!" *However, some of them paid no attention to Moses; they kept part of it until morning, but it was full of maggots and began to smell. So Moses was angry with them.* (Exodus 16:20). When people disobeyed God's instructions their good manna went bad.

Even if you are in the wilderness and running out of supplies, God will provide manna from heaven to sustain you if you follow instructions.

Chapter 13

Things that Are Not

Therefore, the promise comes by faith, so that it may be by grace and may be guaranteed to all Abraham's offspring--not only to those who are of the law but also to those who are of the faith of Abraham. He is the father of us all. As it is written: "I have made you a father of many nations." He is our father in the sight of God, in whom he believed--the God who gives life to the dead and calls things that are not as though they were. Against all hope, Abraham in hope believed and so became the father of many nations, just as it had been said to him, "So shall your offspring be." (Romans 4:16-18).

The end of the year is often a day of frustration and exasperation. If we could stand on the horizon and push back the rising sun on this day we would rush to the edge of the world and shout, "STOP!" It is a time when we take inventory and invariably think of the things that are NOT. We did not get our promotion. In fact, we did not keep our job. We did not find the man or woman who is going to fulfill our lives. We did not stop foreclosure. We did not...

Be assured that if we can't remember the things that are not, someone else will remind us. I recently encountered a young man who was loudly criticizing the church while complaining about what the church is not. He argued that churches are not part of the communities in which they are located and they are not interested in

anything except money. He didn't allow facts to get in
the way of his opinions. He was unmoved by the fact
that over 19,000 families that do not belong to the church
have been fed since the inception of the food pantry
ministry. He was determined to declare the things that
are not.

Paul writes that Abraham's faith was in a God
who could do two amazing things: (1) give life to the
dead and (2) call things that are not as though they were.
We need to be reminded that Abraham's initial reaction
to the promise of God was doubt and laughter. Not only
that, he also tried to develop a human plan to accomplish
God's divine promise. *Abraham fell face down; he laughed
and said to himself, "Will a son be born to a man a hundred
years old? Will Sarah bear a child at the age of ninety?" And
Abraham said to God, "if only Ishmael might live under your
blessing!"* (Genesis 17:17-18). Abraham knew that he and
Sarah were not young. In fact, they were physically as
good as dead. *Without weakening in his faith, he faced the
fact that his body was as good as dead--since he was about a
hundred years old--and that Sarah's womb was also dead.*
(Mark 4:19).

Abraham did not see how this could happen but
he obviously believed that if it did it would be because he
and Sarah made it happen. God may be great, Abraham
probably thought, but he cannot call the dead to life.
That's why he asked that the promise might be fulfilled
through Ishmael since he and Sarah had arranged that
matter with their slave, Hagar. Abraham kept wondering
how these things could be while trying to apply his weak
human mind to the impossible task of trying to figure out
the miraculous. He and his wife did not readily stop
their human engineering and simply put their trust in the
promises of God. Yet, they found that God can indeed
give life to the dead.

They kept focusing on things that are not. This is a problem of most denominational churches. We focus so much on what is not that we forget or even laugh at the God who is able to call the things that are not as though they were. Paul praises Abraham for his faith. The writer of Hebrews cites Abraham's faith as the source of his righteousness. They fail to mention that skepticism and doubt preceded faith. Abraham eventually came to faith but only after he had a good laugh about the things that were not.

We see what is not. God declares what will be. *"I revealed myself to those who did **not** ask for me; I was found by those who did **not** seek me. To a nation that did **not** call on my name, I said, "Here am I, here am I."* (Isaiah 65:1). We invite those who are not part of the household of faith to accept the Christ who revealed himself two thousand years ago. It's time to take inventory and list the things that are not and then take that list to *the God who gives life to the dead and calls things that are not as though they were.*

Even if the world declares the things that are not, keep the faith in the God who is able.

Chapter 14

My Redeemer Lives

I know that my Redeemer lives, and that in the end he will stand upon the earth. (Job 19:25).

But he knows the way that I take; when he has tested me, I will come forth as gold. (Job 23:10).

I find myself thinking a lot lately about why the righteous suffer. It's not because I feel so holy and complain about my minor aches and pains. It just seems that so many innocent people have fallen victim to the actions of very evil people. Sometimes they are little children who haven't lived long enough to harm anyone or some saintly missionary worker or evangelist who is tortured and tormented by an atheistic or anti-Christian government.

There was a time when the angels, including the fallen angels, came to report to God. It is interesting to note that God continued to have dialogue with the angels who rebelled and were thrown out of heaven. God asked them to account for what they had been doing. Satan's answer was similar to that from many who were up to no good, "nothing in particular. I'm just walking around to see what's what." Then the Lord bragged on Job. *"Have you considered my servant Job?"* (Job 1:8). I imagine that we would all like to live so well that God would call us as the parade example to present to the devil as he traveled back and forth on the earth. However, when I consider what happened to Job, I am not so sure. Satan got God's permission to take all of Job's stuff, his toys and even his family. But he was not given permission to touch his body. Then Satan went out from the presence of the LORD. Satan had God's permission to do this horrible work, but he could not do it in God's presence.

This is one of the most challenging theological ideas. Why does God permit bad things to happen to good people, especially to those who are of the household of faith? Sometimes bad things happen to an individual because that individual went into Job's house, or got on Job's bus, or drove across Job's bridge. Satan had God's permission to mess with Job and all that was part of his household. The devil unleashed an attack and destroyed everything that Job possessed; all of the livestock, the slaves and his children. Job gave his famous stoic reply that is as powerful as it is puzzling, *"Naked I came from my mother's womb, and naked I will depart. The LORD gave and the LORD has taken away; may the name of the LORD be praised."* (Job 1:21). This is a very noble reply about the stuff that Job possessed. What about the people, the sons, the daughters, and the slaves? Surely they are worth more than the things that Job lost.

The good news is, that *in all this, Job did not sin by charging God with wrongdoing,* (Job 1:22). There is also bad news. Satan came back. *On another day the angels came to present themselves before the LORD, and Satan also came with them to present himself before him,* (Job 2:1). The devil lost this round and simply upped the ante as he got God to agree that *"Very well, then, he is in your hands; but you must spare his life."* (Job 2:6). At last, the devil had permission to attack Job's body. This attack was vicious and vile. *So Satan went out from the presence of the LORD and afflicted Job with painful sores from the soles of his feet to the top of his head.   Then Job took a piece of broken pottery and scraped himself with it as he sat among the ashes,* (Job 2:7-8).

Job's wife finally lost it. Enough is enough! *His wife said to him, "Are you still holding on to your integrity? Curse God and die!" He replied, "You are talking like a foolish woman. Shall we accept good from God, and not trouble?" In all this, Job did not sin in what he said,* (Job 2:9-10). Job's wife is often vilified for her reaction. However, her response is perhaps the most real of all. The normal human reaction to perceived unfair treatment is to lash out at the one who is responsible and has the power.

His wife was first and his friends were not far behind. *When Job's three friends, Eliphaz the Temanite, Bildad the Shuhite and Zophar the Naamathite, heard about all the troubles that had come upon him, they set out from their homes and met together by agreement to go and sympathize with him and comfort him. When they saw him from a distance, they could hardly recognize him; they began to weep aloud, and they tore their robes and sprinkled dust on their heads. Then they sat on the ground with him for seven days and seven nights. No one said a word to him, because they saw how great his suffering was,* (Job 2:11-13).

It's a real blessing to have friends who can share with you in a time of trouble and torment but no one said a word to him. I can really relate to how Job must have felt. About twelve years ago I found myself the victim of a mysterious ailment that left me feeling sick all of the time. It was not a glamorous manly ailment like a heart attack. My complexion had changed to a constantly ashy look and I just felt sick. The reaction of my friends was the same as Job's friends. They whispered to others about how bad I looked but they did not talk to me. I eventually had surgery to remove the deteriorating gall bladder that was slowly poisoning me. Afterward, I learned Job's lesson about friends.

We often read from Job chapter 19 at funeral interment services: *I know that my Redeemer lives, and that in the end he will stand upon the earth. And after my skin has been destroyed, yet in my flesh I will see God; I myself will see him with my own eyes--I, and not another. How my heart yearns within me!* (Job 19:25-27). This is an amazing prophetic statement coming from the mind of an ancient thinker whose words point to the cross. However, Job's Redeemer may have been someone other than Christ, perhaps the Kinsman Redeemer well known in ancient Jewish thought. To redeem means to "buy back" or to reclaim. Job said that the one who would reclaim his estate was alive and that he would see him with his own eyes even if his skin was destroyed.

Why did God keep telling the devil, *"Have you considered my servant Job?"* Job eventually figured that out himself. *But he knows the way that I take; when he has tested me, I will come forth as gold, (Job 23:10).* God calls your name when the devil comes around because he knows that you will come through the refiner's fire like pure gold. Job not only did not curse God; Job blessed God.

Jesus asked his disciples to remember him when he instituted the sacrament that we now call the Lord's Supper. I am sure that he meant that they should not forget his suffering and his agony. They should remember his pain and his torment. He also meant that when we are in pain, we should remember that Jesus said, *"I have told you these things, so that in me you may have peace. In this world you will have trouble. But take heart! I have overcome the world,"* (John 16:33). We should remember that on the third day our Redeemer arose from the dead so that we can shout with Job, "I know that my Redeemer lives!"

Even if trouble is on every side and friends and family turn away, remember to shout, "I know that my Redeemer lives!"

Chapter 15

Selah

Psalm 46:1-3
God is our refuge and strength,
An ever-present help in trouble.
Therefore we will not fear, though the earth give way
And the mountains fall into the heart of the sea,
Though its waters roar and foam
And the mountains quake with their surging.
Selah

Many years ago I was asked to read the scripture at a district conference worship service. I read Psalm 46 with the usual enthusiasm and reverence. The Presiding Elder called me aside after the service had ended and told me with obvious irritation that I had made the amazing error of reading the word "*Selah*" aloud. "This should never be done!" he exclaimed.

My embarrassment caused me to look into this mysterious word. *Webster's College Dictionary* was of little help, "An expression occurring frequently in the Psalms whose meaning is uncertain; thought to be a liturgical or musical note." *The New Scofield Reference Bible* is a little more certain, "A musical direction, pause." Reverend William Gazaway, the late Presiding Elder of the Dayton District of the A.M.E. Church used to say that Selah meant "pause, but don't quit."

I felt that we should reflect on this psalm and the cryptic musical notation that separates each stanza of the song. Moreover, the three stanzas allow the production of a classic three-point sermon.

God is our refuge and strength, an ever-present help in trouble, (Psalm 46:1).

All fighters for independence, whether political, physical, social or spiritual, need the assurance that comes from an understanding of the role of God in the struggle.   To the young Americans, the British forces must have appeared to be insurmountable. These Americans who longed for their freedom from the British, held other human beings in bondage who longed for liberation and independence.   Surely the first Americans prayed for the freedom to roam the Great Plains once again. Seekers of independence are sustained by the assurance that *God is our refuge and strength.* When the odds seem to be overwhelmingly against us we hear the psalmist singing loudly that God is *an ever-present help in trouble.* And now, having sung the first verses of Psalm 46, we encounter this unfathomable, undefined musical notation, Selah.   While the last note is still ringing in our ear, it causes us to pause to reflect, meditate and let it sink in. God is our refuge! God is our strength! God is our help in trouble!

There is a river whose streams make glad the city of God, the holy place where the Most High dwells. God is within her, she will not fall, (Psalm 46:4-5). Ezekiel had a vision of this river. *The man brought me back to the entrance of the temple and I saw water coming out from under the threshold of the temple toward the east (for the temple faced east). The water was coming down from under the south side of the temple, south of the altar. Fruit trees of all kinds will grow on both banks of the river. Their leaves will not wither, nor will their fruit fail. Every month they will bear, because the water from the sanctuary flows to them. Their fruit will serve for food and their leaves for healing,* (Ezekiel 47:1,12). If God is within this city, within this country, within this church, she will not fall because there is a river through which all supplies come. The banks of the river are lined with life-giving fruit trees that never fail to produce. The leaves of this tree can be applied to blistering sores to bring about healing. Now, (here we go again) *Selah.* Pause, reflect, and meditate on the grace of God. God makes a river of blessings to flow. God is within our midst. We cannot fall. We cannot fail.

Come and see the works of the LORD; *"Be still, and know that I am God,"* (Psalm 46:8, 10).

The psalmist calls us to come and see the works of the Lord. These are not our works. These are not the works of the preacher, the bishop, the generals or the soldiers. The Lord is working. Then God says to us, *"Be still."* In other words, God is saying that when God is working, we should stop our feeble efforts to act like God. Just be still! Sometimes God has to do some very dramatic things in order for us to be still. A very active officer in the church ends up flat on his back in the hospital. He cries out "Why God? Why?" The pastor who thinks that nothing happens without him is surprisingly struck by a debilitating heart condition. He wonders, "How can this be Lord? How can this be?" It may be God's way of reminding us that we were told to *"Be still!"* If we are still, there is no possibility that we might think that we deserve credit for what God is doing.

We can read the same sentence with emphasis on different words and get new meanings from the phrase. If we emphasize *"know"* it means that we have no doubt that God is the able deliverer who meets all of our needs. This is a very valuable lesson. It is important for us to be sure, to know. If, however, we read the same sentence and emphasize "I" we hear God saying loudly and clearly that only God is God. No matter what your position is in life, you are not God. We need to be reminded that the President is not God. Congress is not God. This country is not God. And now for the last time, let us pronounce the unpronounceable and speak the unspeakable, *Selah*! Stop and consider seriously the last verse of the song.

We are not surprised that the disciples ended the last meal where Jesus instituted the Lord's Supper by singing a hymn. *When they had sung a hymn, they went out to the Mount of Olives.* (Matthew 26:30). As Jesus and his disciples went out on the most critical night of their lives, they sang a hymn. The hymn might have been Psalm 114 or some other song in the Hallel, the collection of psalms of praise to God for God's deliverance from danger. There is no Selah in the entire collection. This was no longer a time to pause or hesitate or even meditate and reflect. This was a time to go out and take action.

There was a time when we ended Communion without the usual benediction. We simply sang a hymn and went out. We often sang Elisha Hoffman's inspiring words, "What a fellowship, what a joy divine, leaning on the everlasting arms. What a blessedness what a peace is mine, leaning on the everlasting arms." The disciples had the privilege of leaning on Jesus at the dinner table and now they continued to lean on his strong arms as they went out into the night to deal with the devil.

Even if you step out into your night, don't be afraid, don't hesitate. *God is our refuge and strength, an ever-present help in trouble.*

Chapter 16

Are You Still Hungry?

Jesus said to them, "I tell you the truth, unless you eat the flesh of the Son of Man and drink his blood, you have no life in you," (John 6:53).

Jesus enjoyed a good meal. He was often criticized because he liked to eat and drink so much. He said that others came fasting and they were criticized and he came eating and drinking and he was criticized. He knew that you can't please some people. So, he ignored the complainers and took advantage of the mealtime opportunity to worship, fellowship, and, of course, teach. Jesus' meals always included worship. He prayed, he read the scriptures, and he sang hymns. He worshiped God with thanksgiving and praise.

Mealtime also provided the classroom for Jesus to teach his disciples the hard lessons that they had to learn if they were to follow him all the way to the cross and beyond. Jesus called himself the *"Son of Man."* What did he mean by this term? After all, if he was the Son of God without an earthly father, how could he be the Son of Man? He was not the son of the man Joseph. The Son of Man was predicted, expected, and hoped for. Jesus identified himself as that special man, but he did not present himself in the way that they expected. He came asking them a very strange question: "Are you still hungry?"

Recently I thought that I was hungry. We decided to stop by a restaurant that was well known for its hamburgers. The hamburger and fries looked truly delicious. I drenched them with ketchup as usual and prepared to chow down when my darling wife casually mentioned a letter that was circulating on the internet. It warned against eating ketchup from bottles in restaurants because some evil fiend allegedly was putting blood in the bottles. I don't know why my sweetheart chose that moment to tell me about the emails but suddenly I found that I no longer had an appetite. The good news, though, is that I have a new appreciation for how the disciples must have felt when Jesus made his strange pronouncements about flesh and blood.

Whoever eats my flesh and drinks my blood has eternal life, and I will raise him up at the last day, (John 6:54). Whoever eats this meal *has* eternal life. Jesus put this in the present tense. He did not say that they will have eternal life. It is theirs now, in the present if they consume his body. Their physical life may end until the resurrection, but their eternal life begins at the moment they consume this meal.

For my flesh is real food and my blood is real drink. Whoever eats my flesh and drinks my blood remains in me, and I in him. Just as the living Father sent me and I live because of the Father, so the one who feeds on me will live because of me. This is the bread that came down from heaven. Your forefathers ate manna and died, but he who feeds on this bread will live forever, (John 6:55-58). Jesus said that he is the bread that came from heaven. The disciples thought that manna was the bread from heaven. It miraculously appeared each day and enabled the wandering Israelites to survive. Jesus reminded them, however, that manna sustains you for a little while. But eventually one who feeds on manna still succumbs to the ailments of life and dies. He, however, came from heaven to provide life that never ends. The catch is that you have to eat his flesh and

drink his blood despite the fact that the law says that
many foods are allowed but never can one consume
blood.

He said this while teaching in the synagogue in
Capernaum. On hearing it, many of his disciples said, "This is
a hard teaching. Who can accept it? Aware that his disciples
were grumbling about this, Jesus said to them, "Does this
offend you? What if you see the Son of Man ascend to where he
was before!" (John 6:59-62). In other words, Jesus was
asking them if they needed to see something spectacular
in order to believe. Could they not simply accept his
words? What if they saw another miracle? Many
disciples followed because of the miracles, because of the
spectacular. What if they saw him ascend up into the sky
and return to the Father? Would they believe then? He
didn't wait for their answer. He went on to explain that
their literal-minded misinterpretation of his words
would cause them to fall away. He was asking the
question, "Are you still hungry?"

"The Spirit gives life; the flesh counts for nothing. The
words I have spoken to you are spirit and they are life. Yet
there are some of you who do not believe." For Jesus had known
from the beginning which of them did not believe and who
would betray him. He went on to say, "This is why I told you
that no one can come to me unless the Father has enabled him."
From this time many of his disciples turned back and no longer
followed him, (John 6:63-66). Many people who leave the
church will tell you that they left because they are not
being "fed." Jesus' disciples left because he offered to
feed them and they did not like the menu.

"You do not want to leave too, do you?" Jesus asked the
Twelve, (John 6:67). Jesus turned to his closest disciples.
These are the ones who were with him from the
beginning. They witnessed the miracles up close. They
traveled the same dusty roads and slept on the same

hard mats. They were the ones who slaved to raise the money to keep the mission going, who fried the chicken and cleaned the toilets. They had patched the roof and shoveled the driveway. They had left their businesses, their families, everything to follow Jesus. These would be the ones in the church who had rushed their own personal check to the gas company when they threatened to turn off the gas. They were the trustees who wrote special checks from their personal accounts so that the church bills could be paid.

He wasn't asking those who in a moment of temporary rapture had come running down the aisle to follow Jesus. He wasn't asking those who got caught up in his charismatic preaching and came professing a shallow faith. Those people had already left to follow one of the forty or so pretenders to the heavenly throne. He was asking the ones who had traveled with him through thick and thin, come hell or high water. "What about you? Has your zeal lessened? Has your faith faded? Do you find this meal distasteful? When we started this work you hungered and thirsted after righteousness. Are you still hungry?"

Simon Peter answered him, "Lord, to whom shall we go? You have the words of eternal life. We believe and know that you are the Holy One of God," (John 6:68-69). Why did the close disciples, the twelve, not leave? Other disciples left him and walked with him no more. This was too hard for them to take. They had lost their appetite. Why did Peter and the others stay? It's the same reason that some people today stay with the church when others leave. Jesus gave the answer, *You did not choose me, but I chose you and appointed you to go and bear fruit--fruit that will last. Then the Father will give you whatever you ask in my name.* (John 15:16).

Some people came for the show but they left before dinner. Are you still hungry? You were hungry when you first met the Lord. Are you still hungry? You were ready for the feast when God saved you and lifted you out of the mess you were in. Have you lost your appetite now that you know the menu? Are you still hungry now that you know you must swallow your pride?   Are you still thirsty? Think about William Cowper's compelling words: "There is a fountain filled with blood drawn from Emmanuel's veins. And sinners plunged beneath that flood lose all their guilty stains." Are you in despair? Then Thomas Moore urges you: "Come ye disconsolate, where'er ye languish. Come to the mercy seat, fervently kneel. Earth has no sorrow that heaven cannot heal."   Are you still hungry?   Then, "Come to the feast of love; Come, ever knowing. Earth has no sorrow but heaven can remove."

Even if you are losing your appetite, eat and drink and be filled with life that never ends.

Chapter 17

It's Your Move

"To the angel of the church in Laodicea write: These are the words of the Amen, the faithful and true witness, the ruler of God's creation. I know your deeds, that you are neither cold nor hot. I wish you were either one or the other! So, because you are lukewarm--neither hot nor cold--I am about to spit you out of my mouth." (Revelation 3:14-16).

Laodicea was known for banks, clothing, carpet-making, production of black wool, and a famous eye salve. A message was sent to *the angel of the church in Laodicea,* (Revelation 3:14). The word "angel" could also be translated "messenger", that is, pastor. Pastors and other spiritual leaders must always listen for exhortations from the Spirit. The message, in this instance, is about a fault or shortcoming of the church. What kind of fault would require the attention of the Spirit? Surely someone in the church must be lying, stealing, committing adultery or some other serious crime. Imagine our surprise when we read the charge: *These are the words of the Amen, the faithful and true witness, the ruler of God's creation. I know your deeds, that you are neither cold nor hot. I wish you were either one or the other!* (Revelation 3:14-16). Lord, are you telling us that we are in trouble for being lukewarm? Should we be relieved? Does this mean that God did not notice our more serious sins?

The church is doing what many young people do in school. Have you asked a teenager recently about school? "How are you doing in school? Alright. What's your favorite subject? I don't know." The answers are all about the same, lukewarm and impassive. We are often lukewarm because we don't like the message. Paul's letter to the Colossians gives several examples. *And whatever you do, whether in word or deed, do it all in the name of the Lord Jesus, giving thanks to God the Father through him.* (Colossians 3:17). This sounds alright. Most of us could say amen to that. *Whatever you do, work at it with all your heart, as working for the Lord, not for men.* (Colossians 3:23). This sounds just fine. Most of us don't have a problem with Paul's exhortation to be passionate about what we do for Christ.

The problem is the material between verse 17 and verse 23. *Wives, submit to your husbands, as is fitting in the Lord. Husbands, love your wives and do not be harsh with them. Children, obey your parents in everything, for this pleases the Lord. Fathers, do not embitter your children, or they will become discouraged. Slaves, obey your earthly masters in everything; and do it, not only when their eye is on you and to win their favor, but with sincerity of heart and reverence for the Lord.* (Colossians 3:18-22). Now, there's the problem. Wives are lukewarm in their response because they don't want to submit to their husbands. Husbands are lukewarm because they want to be harsh with their wives if they must. Children are lukewarm because they don't think they should have to obey their parents in everything. And don't get me started about slaves obeying their earthly masters.

There are consequences to being lukewarm. God does not like the taste of lukewarm drink. *So, because you are lukewarm--neither hot nor cold--I am about to spit you out of my mouth.* (Revelation 3:16). People who are lukewarm think that they have everything all together. They don't need anything or anybody. *You say, 'I am rich; I have acquired wealth and do not need a thing.' But you do not realize that you are wretched, pitiful, poor, blind and naked.* (Revelation 3:17).

Jesus says that they don't really have it all together. In fact, they don't even have the thing that they are most proud of — the special salve that cures eye diseases. *I counsel you to buy from me gold refined in the fire, so you can become rich; and white clothes to wear, so you can cover your shameful nakedness; and salve to put on your eyes, so you can see.* (Revelation 3:18). Furthermore, Jesus says that you have to learn how to take criticism. A coach doesn't bother criticizing a player who is mediocre and can't do any better. But the one who has the potential to be a superstar is one of, *Those whom I love I rebuke and discipline. So be earnest, and repent.* (Revelation 3:19). Repent means to change your mind and try to do your very best. IT'S YOUR MOVE!

Jesus is tired of the passive, lukewarm church. He says that he is standing at the door and knocking. But, it's your move. He is not going to open the door. It's your move. *Here I am! I stand at the door and knock. If anyone hears my voice and opens the door, I will come in and eat with him, and he with me. To him who overcomes, I will give the right to sit with me on my throne, just as I overcame and sat down with my Father on his throne.* (Revelation 3:20-21).

Even if it is dangerous to take a stand, repent, step out on faith and witness for God.

Chapter 18

Upside-Down Religion

And when they found them not, they drew Jason and certain brethren unto the rulers of the city, crying, These that have turned the world upside down are come hither also; Whom Jason hath received: and these all do contrary to the decrees of Caesar, saying that there is another king, one Jesus. And they troubled the people and the rulers of the city, when they heard these things. And when they had taken security of Jason, and of the other, they let them go. (Acts 17:6-9 KJV).

The book of Acts records a time when Paul, Silas and their companions came into a town preaching the good news about a Savior named Jesus. This was a town that had some people who readily received the news and rejoiced to know that times were changing. But, the town also had some who were very distressed to think that their lifestyle had to change. Paul, after all, taught that there was "no slave or free in Christ." This was not welcome theology in a society where there were as many slaves as free people. They had the nerve to teach that *"God is no respecter of persons."* Once again, those in the upper levels of society did not want to hear such heresies.

So the distressed leaders sent out mobs to try to find Paul, Silas, and the others. *And when they found them not, they drew Jason and certain brethren unto the rulers of the city, crying, These that have turned the world upside down are come hither also,* (Acts 17:6). Who would have known that the racists of the last century were merely quoting the

Bible with their plaintiff cries? I also wonder if they knew that the ancient Hebrew Scriptures also spoke prophesies about a time when God would turn things upside down.

Long before Martin Luther King, Jr. was born, long before Lincoln signed the Emancipation Proclamation, centuries before John Newton discovered God's Amazing Grace, God was shown to be the true God, *Which executeth judgment for the oppressed: which giveth food to the hungry. The LORD looseth the prisoners: The LORD openeth the eyes of the blind: the LORD raiseth them that are bowed down: the LORD loveth the righteous: The LORD preserveth the strangers; he relieveth the fatherless and widow: but the way of the wicked he turneth upside down.* (Psalm 146:7-9 KJV).

Not only did the psalmist prophesy this earth-turning event, so did the Prophet Isaiah. *Behold, the LORD maketh the earth empty, and maketh it waste, and turneth it upside down, and scattereth abroad the inhabitants thereof.* (Isaiah 24:1). It was fore-ordained that the segregated, discriminatory societies had to change. God had decreed that it would be so centuries earlier. The right circumstances plus the arrival of certain godly men and women released the prophesied action.

Notice, however, that the scriptures don't just talk about the effect of Paul's arrival. He and his companions were blamed for much of the upheaval, but so was a local resident named Jason. Jason and the other local supporters of Paul were arrested and then released on bail. It appears that Jason was a recent convert to Christianity. He might have been a Jew named Joshua who took the Greek name Jason when he was converted to the new faith. It is likely that he shared with Paul the experience of having his world turned upside down.

Paul went from persecutor to propagator; from

witness to death to witness to new birth; from defender of status quo to defender of the faith. He had an encounter with Jesus that turned his world upside down. Even modern-day leaders knew that their work could not succeed without the brave efforts of local men and women who would prepare the way for their coming and remain in the community after they left. For that reason, the brave Jasons of the world need to be honored. They were arrested, their houses were burned, they and their families were attacked and even killed. Yet, after Paul left, they stayed and continued the fight.

This reminds me of the time of the bus and consumer boycotts in my hometown in Florida. Local ministers and community leaders provided churches for organizational meetings, drivers for the cars that replaced the boycotted buses and money for gas and other expenses. Words of encouragement and unity went forth from the pulpits of every denomination. The consequence was that the world was turned upside down. No one rode the bus until the first Black drivers were hired and people could ride with dignity and sit anywhere on the bus. No one shopped at the grocery store until some African-American employees were hired. I was able to pay my college tuition because the owners of the major grocery store realized that we would no longer buy groceries from a store that would not allow African-Americans to work to earn the grocery money. Outside leaders like Dr. King encouraged us. But it was Jason and his companions who made it work.

The King Holiday is one of the most controversial holidays celebrated in the United States because it reminds so many people of a time when some people shook things up so that they turned the world upside down. Why was there such alarm that people were coming to turn their world upside down? Did they have a great violent army that would decimate the population? Would they change their world by installing a dictator who would mandate changes in their world? Were violent revolutionaries coming who would overthrow the government by force? Or was something going on here that was even more frightening to those in power? This more frightening thing would cause the most powerful man in America, J. Edgar Hoover, to declare that a non-violent man like Dr. Martin Luther King was "the most dangerous Negro in America." What was dangerous about a scholarly preacher who didn't carry a weapon and talked about peace? What was dangerous about the Apostle Paul with his weak eyes, small stature and peculiar appearance?

Hoover knew how the right-side-up world worked. He could intimidate the most powerful men in the country so that they re-appointed him year after year. He had the pictures, the tapes, the files of all of their indiscretions. All was right-side-up with the world. Then a man came along like King, in the tradition of Paul and turned everything upside down. How did he do it? It was not by being perfect. He was a flawed human being. I realize the redundancy in that statement. Suffice it to say he was human. That he was flawed comes with that designation. How then, did he cause the world to alter the spin of its axis and re-orient itself? He did it because he, like Paul called on his brothers and sisters to repent. Repent does not mean to simply be sorry. It means to change your mind. These men turned the world upside down because they were calling on people to change their mind about God.

The most important change was that they had to stop worshiping the god they created and begin to worship the God who created them. This is a radical change—too radical for most American Christians. I had a professor once who used to ask the class who had found any nuggets in the scripture. He said that a nugget was a special truth about God revealed through our studies and meditation. In other words, this knowledge of God was like pure gold. So many of us take the golden nuggets of biblical truth and cast them into the fires of doubt, of prejudice, of racism, of gender bias, and of exploitation. I am glad that every now and then God sends a Paul to stand in the midst of the idol worshipers and turn their world upside down.

When God turns our world upside down, God is really putting things back the way that they once were. The Bible tells us that God created *"and it was good."* (Genesis 1:23-24; 31). This *"good"* world was turned upside down when *"man"* and *"woman"* decided to disobey God and do things their way. The world remained in that state until Jesus came, died and rose again. When Paul came preaching Jesus—the real Jesus—people got upset. They were so used to living in an upside-down world with the gods they created that looked, smelled and acted like them that they couldn't stand the idea that they had to repent.

Here's the good news. Not only does God call us to repent, but God makes it possible. All we have to do is abandon those gods that we created and worship the God of the universe who says simply *"I Am who I Am."* Worship God, not an idol. Worship and believe Christ, not an empty image. Then your world will begin to rotate slowly, so that you won't lose your balance. It will move slowly, so that you regain perspective. Slowly, your world will be turned upside down and become right again with God.

Even if you are living with injustice, worship God and believe Christ and your world will become right again.

Chapter 19

On Fire But Not Burnt Out

When his father-in-law saw all that Moses was doing for the people, he said, "What is this you are doing for the people? Why do you alone sit as judge, while all these people stand around you from morning till evening?" Moses answered him, "Because the people come to me to seek God's will. Whenever they have a dispute, it is brought to me, and I decide between the parties and inform them of God's decrees and laws." Moses' father-in-law replied, "What you are doing is not good. You and these people who come to you will only wear yourselves out. The work is too heavy for you; you cannot handle it alone." (Exodus 18:14-18).

We recently had a wedding at my church. Weddings are wonderful events. This one was especially nice. The bride was beautiful, the groom was nervously anxious and the in-laws were relieved. All was right with the world. Weddings make you think of mothers-in-law but this scripture is about a meddling father-in-law. Many strange and incorrect images of biblical characters come from the movies. We saw Charlton Heston as Moses boldly confronting Pharaoh. Moses was a great leader but the Bible makes it clear that he had flaws. He was not perfect. He could not speak well. Aaron was actually the articulate spokesman. Moses was a father and family man who fathered at least two sons with his wife Zipporah. It appears that he got so involved in his work that he sent his wife and sons home to her father's house. Jethro, the father-in-law was a priest of Midian who thought he knew how to worship his god, no matter what his idea of God may have been. He is the one who would have made the sacrifices on behalf of his people and led them in the process of pleasing their gods.

Jethro must have been proud of his son-in-law, the great big shot leader of the Israeli people and a former prince of Egypt. His daughter had married well. Imagine his excitement when he had a chance to visit Moses and watch him work. My father-in-law died four years before I married his daughter, so I don't know how I would have felt if he had come to visit me at my workplace. I suspect that any groom would feel a little nervous under those conditions, especially if the father-in-law was in the same business. Moses was a religious leader. So was Jethro.

Jethro was delighted to hear about all the good things the LORD had done for Israel in rescuing them from the hand of the Egyptians. He said, "Praise be to the LORD, who rescued you from the hand of the Egyptians and of Pharaoh, and who rescued the people from the hand of the Egyptians. Now I know that the LORD is greater than all other gods, for he did this to those who had treated Israel arrogantly," (Exodus 18:9-11). Jethro's mention of other gods indicates that he may have been a henotheist instead of a monotheist. Henotheists were essentially polytheists who believed that they had a special god while not denying the existence of other gods for other people. Many of us today use henotheistic language in our own praise and worship services. If you don't believe it, consider the lyrics of a popular song, "God is *a* good God, He's a great God. He can do anything but fail." I know that the songwriter intends only the highest praise and respect for God. However, I am sure that the theological point that they are trying to make is not that God is *a* good God, but that God is good.

God is the only God. God is great, not merely *a great God*. Jethro realized that God is great when he heard of all that God had done for the Israelites. Notice that even Jethro recognized that the praise should go to God, not Moses. He joined with Aaron and the other priests in sacrificing to God. The glory belonged to God.

Then, the big moment came and Jethro got to observe Moses in action as the leader of his people. *The next day Moses took his seat to serve as judge for the people, and they stood around him from morning till evening. When his father-in-law saw all that Moses was doing for the people, he said, "What is this you are doing for the people? Why do you alone sit as judge, while all these people stand around you from morning till evening?" Moses answered him, "Because the people come to me to seek God's will. Whenever they have a dispute, it is brought to me, and I decide between the parties and inform them of God's decrees and laws." Moses' father-in-law replied, "What you are doing is not good. You and these people who come to you will only wear yourselves out. The work is too heavy for you; you cannot handle it alone."* (Exodus 18:13-18). Jethro was alarmed by Moses' one man show. He knew that this was a prescription for burnout before the term had been invented.

Listen now to me and I will give you some advice, and may God be with you. You must be the people's representative before God and bring their disputes to him. Teach them the decrees and laws, and show them the way to live and the duties they are to perform. But select capable men from all the people-- men who fear God, trustworthy men who hate dishonest gain-- and appoint them as officials over thousands, hundreds, fifties and tens. Have them serve as judges for the people at all times, but have them bring every difficult case to you; the simple cases they can decide themselves. That will make your load lighter, because they will share it with you. If you do this and God so commands, you will be able to stand the strain, and all these people will go home satisfied, (Exodus 18:19-23). The advice worked because *Moses listened to his father-in-law and did everything he said,* (Exodus 18:24).

Jesus affirmed these principles many years later when he fed the hungry multitudes. Note how he involved the disciples in the miracle. Jesus had the power to supply all of the food needed by the gathered crowd that had come to hear him preach, but he had told the disciples to feed them. They made excuses and failed to carry out his command. Jesus did not let them off the hook. He did not simply wave his hand and have manna fall from heaven though he obviously had that power and ability. Instead, he told the disciples to do two things. First, take inventory and see what you have. Jesus knew what was there. He wanted the disciples to know that they should first take stock of their supplies before they declared that there was not enough to meet the needs of the people. John indicates that they only found a small amount of food in a little boy's lunch. *"Here is a boy with five small barley loaves and two small fish, but how far will they go among so many?"* (John 6:9). That was not enough in the opinion of the disciples to feed so many people. They must have thought Jesus would come to his senses when he considered the facts. Surely now he would send someone into town to get some food. Jesus showed them that the amount of the supplies was not the issue. They needed to trust God to provide *even if* God had to start with nothing as when God spoke the world into existence.

Second, he made them organize the people into manageable groups. It is hard to serve people if you just see them as one large, faceless mass without personalities, resources or intellects. *Jesus said, "Have the people sit down." There was plenty of grass in that place, and the men sat down, about five thousand of them,* (John 6:10).

Organize them so that you can see who they are and they can see you in your active role in support of Jesus. *Jesus then took the loaves, gave thanks, and distributed to those who were seated as much as they wanted. He did the same with the fish,* (John 6:11). The New King James translation is even more explicit about how Jesus distributed the food. *And Jesus took the loaves, and when He had given thanks He distributed them to the disciples, and the disciples to those sitting down; and likewise of the fish, as much as they wanted,* (John 6:11). The point is that he involved the disciples. He gave them the food and the disciples gave the food to the people. The people saw that the disciples worked with Jesus to perform this amazing miracle.

Some of you may be thinking that this is all very interesting but that it is a bit of a stretch to relate the administrative work of Moses to the ministry of Jesus and his disciples. However, that is exactly what Jesus did right before he performed this miracle. Jesus was engaged in a contentious argument with the Pharisees about his authority and the authority of Moses whom they revered. *"But do not think I will accuse you before the Father. Your accuser is Moses, on whom your hopes are set. If you believed Moses, you would believe me, for he wrote about me. But since you do not believe what he wrote, how are you going to believe what I say?"* (John 5:45-47).

All of this leads to the only point of this chapter: you don't have to *burn out to be on fire for the Lord.* Many servants of God find themselves overwhelmed and burnt out trying to respond to all that God seems to require them to do. Jeremiah described this urging of God as a "fire" in his bones. You should be so zealous to serve God that people sense the fire in your spirit. But, you can't do any good thing for God if you are burnt up and burnt out. Jethro brought the message to Moses and Jesus taught the lesson to his disciples. (1) Take inventory. Look at the resources that God has already given you to apply toward the problem. (2) Organize the people and develop a plan to meet their needs. (3) Thank God for what you have. (4) Have your helpers join you in distributing God's blessings.

At that time Jesus, full of joy through the Holy Spirit, said, "I praise you, Father, Lord of heaven and earth, because you have hidden these things from the wise and learned, and revealed them to little children. Yes, Father, for this was your good pleasure." All things have been committed to me by my Father. No one knows who the Son is except the Father, and no one knows who the Father is except the Son and those to whom the Son chooses to reveal him." Then he turned to his disciples and said privately, "Blessed are the eyes that see what you see. For I tell you that many prophets and kings wanted to see what you see but did not see it, and to hear what you hear but did not hear it." (Luke 10:21-24).

Jesus was filled with joy by the Holy Spirit who empowered him to be obedient all the way to the cross and death. He explained to the disciples how blessed they were to be able to experience what so many prophets before had longed to see. They received lessons in how to work miracles from the great miracle worker himself. They not only saw his actions. They saw his energy. He got physically tired sometimes but never weary of his journey. He honored them by allowing them to share in his glory even as he anticipated his suffering. James Cleveland sang it as only he could, "I don't feel no ways tired. Nobody told me the road would be easy. I don't believe he brought me this far to leave me."

Even if the problem seems to be great, if I just look around me with the eyes of faith I will see that the little that I have is the starting material for God to work a great miracle. If I break the big problem down into manageable parts, solutions are possible. We can be on fire for the Lord without getting burnt out.

Chapter 20

After the Storm

Again he said, "What shall we say the kingdom of God is like, or what parable shall we use to describe it? It is like a mustard seed, which is the smallest seed you plant in the ground. Yet when planted, it grows and becomes the largest of all garden plants, with such big branches that the birds of the air can perch in its shade." With many similar parables Jesus spoke the word to them, as much as they could understand. He did not say anything to them without using a parable. But when he was alone with his own disciples, he explained everything. (Mark 4:30-34).

Jesus spent a lot of time trying to explain himself to his followers. He was a master teacher who knew how to use examples and illustrations from the everyday lives of his disciples. Some tended sheep and some were farmers so he often used pastoral scenes in his homilies. Everyone had to deal with tax collectors, judges and other people in power who often made their way into his stories.

So, Jesus used an ancient rabbinical method called the parable as his primary instructional tool. Jesus' explanation for using parables is somewhat obscure because he quoted a cryptic declaration from Isaiah 6:10 when he said, *the knowledge of the secrets of the kingdom of God has been given to you, but to others I speak in parables, so that, "though seeing, they may not see; though hearing, they may not understand."* (Luke 8:10). He might have been suggesting that those who are not true disciples would not apprehend the message while believers would eventually come to faith and a true understanding.

Jesus had declared that the kingdom of God was at hand but few seemed to understand what he meant by that so he presented his message using a parable. *Again he said, "What shall we say the kingdom of God is like, or what parable shall we use to describe it? It is like a mustard seed, which is the smallest seed you plant in the ground. Yet when planted, it grows and becomes the largest of all garden plants, with such big branches that the birds of the air can perch in its shade."* (Mark 4:30-32). What did Jesus mean by this? What is this *smallest seed* that when planted grows to become the largest of all? I believe that it was the simple idea expressed in the most basic words possible—*God so loved the world.* That is, the kingdom of God is based on a small thing called love that starts in our hearts and grows. The residents of the kingdom of God are required only to have an abiding faith in the love of God that is expressed through Jesus Christ. Worldly kingdoms are built on power, fear, military might and intimidation. This is not surprising since few ancient theologians had developed the idea that deities had feelings of love toward mankind.

In another parable Jesus talked about the mystery of the kingdom's growth. It is imperceptible; it is hidden from visual observation but persistent. *He also said, "This is what the kingdom of God is like. A man scatters seed on the ground. Night and day, whether he sleeps or gets up, the seed sprouts and grows, though he does not know how. All by itself the soil produces grain—first the stalk, then the head, then the full kernel in the head."* (Mark 4:26-28). This kingdom could not be stopped by human action or inaction. God is sovereign and the kingdom of God is that place where the perfect will of God rules.

This discussion of parables and Jesus' desire to teach his slow-witted disciples might help us to understand fully the famous incident that follows. *That day when evening came, he said to his disciples, "Let us go over to the other side." Leaving the crowd behind, they took him along, just as he was, in the boat. There were also other boats with him.* (Mark 4:35-36). Jesus sometimes calls his disciples to go over to the other side. He had preached and taught on this side. He had healed the people on this side. Some of them had not learned the lesson of the day, but he loved them anyway. He was not calling his disciples to abandon those on this side. He was urging them to carry his message into new territories. Be assured that Jesus also knew that getting to the other side would provide a new opportunity to teach his closest disciples the lessons that they had to learn if they were going to do kingdom work.

A furious squall came up, and the waves broke over the boat, so that it was nearly swamped. (Mark 4:37). The first lesson that Jesus taught was that even when we are on a mission assigned by Jesus himself, we still can encounter storms. All of the boats in the armada were being tossed about by some very rough waves. This was a sudden and unexpected development. After all, what could be more secure than traveling with Jesus? They were obviously frightened by the storm but they were clearly irritated by Jesus' casual attitude. The expected reaction when storms come is hysteria and panic. Jesus wanted to teach his disciples that with Christ, there is another way. As they crossed to the other side, they needed an attitude adjustment if they were going to be successful in their mission. Jesus showed that he had complete faith in his heavenly Father. He slept peacefully while they were frantically flailing about in fear.

Jesus was in the stern, sleeping on a cushion. The disciples woke him and said to him, "Teacher, don't you care if we drown?" (Mark 4:38). Jesus wanted to be sure that the disciples did not think that he had merely dozed off for a short nap. He took a pillow and made himself comfortable as he slept. His calm demeanor caused the disciples to accuse him of not caring. This reminds me of a common reaction at funerals where the observers determine the love of the family for the deceased by the volume of noisy wailing and moaning coming from the bereaved family. In truth, sometimes the one expressing the loudest grief is the one who has the greatest regret about missed opportunities for service while the person was still living. Those who seized every moment to embrace the ones they loved while they were still alive can quietly and reverently reflect on the love they shared.

Jesus did not respond to the complaint from his disciples. *He got up, rebuked the wind and said to the waves, "Quiet! Be still!" Then the wind died down and it was completely calm.* (Mark 4:39). He then proceeded to teach them the lesson. *He said to his disciples, "Why are you so afraid? Do you still have no faith?" They were terrified and asked each other, "Who is this? Even the wind and the waves obey him!"* (Mark 4:40-41). Did you notice that while they were very unsettled by the storm they were *terrified* by the calm that followed when Jesus spoke a word of peace to the wind and the waves? They cowered before the fury of an indifferent and deadly nature. They had never seen a man who could speak to the wind and have it obey.

They then asked themselves the question—the only question—on the final examination given by Professor Jesus: *Who is this?* Remember, these were not casual followers. These were his closest disciples who were chosen directly by Jesus. They had every reason to believe that they knew him. But, until that point, they like the other followers may have been hanging with Jesus because of the miracles while knowing that other charismatic leaders had also performed apparent miracles. It was possible to coerce or hypnotize or bribe men and women into pretending to have been healed from an ailment or disability. But the elements could not be induced to respond to a man's command. Only God could speak to the wind and the waves.

Who is this? Do you know him? Has he spoken to the storms in your life? Have you experienced the calm, not with fear but with reverence? Do you know that he is holy, mighty, and loving?

Even if storms come into our lives, Jesus is the master of the winds and the waves and will speak a word of peace if we put our trust in him.

Chapter 21

Bread Corn Is Bruised

Then he asked them, "Who do you say I am?" Simon Peter answered, "You are the Messiah, the Son of the living God." (Matthew 16:16).

For the fitches are not threshed with a threshing instrument, neither is a cart wheel turned about upon the cummin; but the fitches are beaten out with a staff, and the cummin with a rod. Bread corn is bruised; because he will not ever be threshing it, nor break it with the wheel of his cart, nor bruise it with his horsemen. This also cometh forth from the LORD of hosts, which is wonderful in counsel, and excellent in working. (Isaiah 28:27-29, KJV).

Jesus asked his gathered disciples *"What do they say? Who do they say that I am?"* Can you imagine the uncertainty of the disciples? This is a loaded question. Sometime later, two disillusioned disciples said to the unrecognized resurrected Jesus *"We had hoped that he was the one..."* These disciples had to wonder whether to express their hope, or offer tentative responses to see which one Jesus would accept. *"Some people say, Jesus, that you are John the Baptist brought back to life."* I can see them looking anxiously at Jesus to gauge his response. Nothing. *"Some say Elijah."* No reaction. *"Some say Jeremiah..."* Nope. *"Or one of the other prophets."* This was perhaps as much a question as a statement. Once again, there was no reaction from Jesus.

Jesus was now more direct. *"Who do you say that I*

am?" There was no wiggle room now. No trial balloons could be floated. No tentative responses could be proffered. Peter blurted out the answer. He might have been startled to hear his own exclamation, *"You are the Messiah, the Son of the living God!"* His surprise would not have come because he didn't believe what he said. He fully believed it. He was convinced that Jesus possessed power that could only belong to the Holy One of God. But Peter seemed surprised that he dared to express aloud what they had earnestly longed for in their hearts. He heard himself blurt it out in his characteristically bold way. *"You are the Christ!"*

This famous scripture records the single greatest theological statement given in the New Testament. It is not surprising that this statement came from Simon Peter. He was in a way, like this author, a jackleg preacher. He was unschooled, coarse and vulgar. One translation describes him as *"ignorant and unlearned."* The reverend doctors of today would certainly declare that he was no theologian. Yet, it was he who made this profound theological pronouncement.

Matthew tells us that Jesus told Peter that he was truly blessed because God had given him this great insight. This did not come from his human understanding. He did not figure this out by himself. This great theological truth came in a blessed moment of revelation from God. *Jesus replied, "You are blessed, Simon son of John, because my Father in heaven has revealed this to you. You did not learn this from any human being. Now I say to you that you are Peter, and upon this rock I will build my church, and all the powers of hell will not conquer it."* (Matthew 16:17-18).

Jesus' reaction is fascinating and informative. He could have said "Simon, son of John, you are brilliant." After all, Peter was the one who figured this out. He could have said "Simon, son of John, you are bold. That's what we need to herald the coming kingdom of God—boldness." Peter is the one who moved beyond the uncertainty and timidity of the others. He was audacious enough to shout *"You are the Christ."* He didn't talk about Peter's brilliance. Jesus didn't mention Peter's boldness. Instead he declared *"Peter, you are blessed!"* Blessed. That's a marvelous thought. When God allows us to see clearly and proclaim a great theological truth, we are not brilliant or bold, but blessed.

From then on Jesus began to tell his disciples plainly that he had to go to Jerusalem, and he told them what would happen to him there. He would suffer at the hands of the leaders and the leading priests and the teachers of religious law. He would be killed, and he would be raised on the third day. But Peter took him aside and corrected him. "Heaven forbid, Lord," he said. "This will never happen to you!" Jesus turned to Peter and said, "Get away from me, Satan! You are a dangerous trap to me. You are seeing things merely from a human point of view, and not from God's." (Matthew 16:21-25).

Everything was now out in the open. The "Messianic Secret" was secret no more. At least, it was not secret to the disciples. So, Jesus began to tell the disciples the rest of the story. *He is the Messiah and, therefore, he must be tortured, murdered and raised from the dead.* This was not easy for the disciples to hear. They had just heard Peter's pronouncement and had only a few moments to revel in the fact that they were so close to the one who was promised so long ago. They were so close to the possessor of ultimate power and prestige. They wanted a part of his exaltation, not his humiliation. So, we are not shocked that the same disciple who made the great declaration rushed to challenge Jesus' statement. In a show of extreme arrogance he *corrected*

Jesus. *"Heaven forbid, Lord!"* Peter yelled. Perhaps it was love that made Peter cry out. Perhaps the horrible images of the last crucifixion that he witnessed rushed to the forefront of his mind. Maybe the shameful pictures of nakedness, exposure and brutal humiliation lingered in his consciousness. We don't know. But we do know that the human nature of Peter pushed aside the divine urging that led to his messianic declaration and allowed his sinful human inclinations to rush to the fore. *"This will never happen to you!"*

Jesus rebuked Peter. He didn't do it kindly and gently. He used strong words like those that he had used once before in the wilderness after his greatest initial trial. *"Get thee behind me, Satan!"* He told Peter that he was just like the devil, the great adversary and accuser whose greatest weapon was doubt and strongest strategy was to dissuade. The devil who said "if you are who you say you are, God will not allow harm to come to you. He will send a legion of angels to protect you." It is not surprising that within five verses of Peter's great theological statement, Jesus said to him "You are just like the devil. Get away from me."

Christians need to pay close attention to this pericope of scripture. There are times when we are blessed by God to be able to speak with special insight, due to the power of the Holy Spirit who chooses to use us for a moment to speak great theological truths. Sometimes this happens in sermonic form. Sometimes God allows us to speak in such a way that others understand the *"marvelous works of God."* (Acts 2:2). So often, these blessed moments are followed quickly by our ego-driven pronouncements that satisfy self and not God. It is then that we realize that Christ's rebuke of Peter is intended for all who would insert their human will into the divine plan of God.

Peter's horror at the thought of what might happen to Jesus had to become subordinate to God's design for the saving work of Christ. Christ's strong reaction to Peter was surely driven by his perfect understanding of the sacrificial nature of his life and death. Isaiah had recorded it in *Isaiah 28:28.* "*Bread corn is bruised; because he will not ever be threshing it, nor break it with the wheel of his cart, nor bruise it with his horsemen.*" Sometimes when we are bruised in life, it is because we are bread corn. When Jesus described himself as the Bread of Life he knew the words of *Isaiah 53:10. Yet it pleased the* LORD *to bruise him; he hath put him to grief: when thou shalt make his soul an offering for sin.* The Authorized Version expresses it in such powerful language: *But he was wounded for our transgressions, he was bruised for our iniquities: the chastisement of our peace was upon him; and with his stripes we are healed.* (Isaiah 53:5).

Even if we feel bruised and abused and it seems that God is allowing the abuse, we should remember that all of this comes from the Lord who has wonderful plans for us. God may be making bread. Bread corn cannot be prepared for baking unless it is *bruised*.